TEN GENERATIONS

TEN
GENERATIONS

A family story from rags to riches

MARK LOWCOCK

Matador
9 Priory Business Park,
Wistow Road, Kibworth Beauchamp,
Leicestershire. LE8 0RX
Tel: 0116 279 2299
Email: books@troubador.co.uk
Web: www.troubador.co.uk/matador
Twitter: @matadorbooks

ISBN 978 1800461 291

British Library Cataloguing in Publication Data.
A catalogue record for this book is available from the British Library.

Printed and bound by CPI Group (UK) Ltd, Croydon, CR0 4YY
Typeset in 11pt Adobe Caslon Pro by Troubador Publishing Ltd, Leicester, UK

Matador is an imprint of Troubador Publishing Ltd

To Dom, Jonathan and Helena

And also to Gemma, Emanuel, Fred,
Amy, George, Alessia and Hannah
because half of this is your story too.

Contents

Where They Lived

Preface

Names, dates, places, events and other things presented as fact in what follows are accurate to the best of my knowledge. Where I have made assumptions, judgements, guesses or inferences, that is made clear.

Our story includes 120 main characters, and touches on many more. The main characters are, for ease of reference, listed in the Appendix at the end.

1

Rags: The Sixteenth and Seventeenth Centuries

---

in which we meet the Mocks of Baden-Württemberg
and the Lowcocks of Skipton, and speculate
about your ancestors from the Lake District,
Northumberland, Ireland, Wales and elsewhere.

Your great-great-great-great-great-great-great-great-great-grandfather, Balthasar Mock, had a problem. Baden-Württemberg was a catastrophe. He had to get out of there. But how? And where to? Just to the east of the Black Forest – from where the German cherry-and-chocolate cake originates – the region of Baden-Württemberg now enjoys picturesque valleys, wooded slopes, steep vineyards and rugged cliffs. Balthasar's grandparents, Lenhart and Apolonia Mock, born in Bopfingen, a small town in Baden-Württemberg, had lived there from the middle of the sixteenth century. So did their son, Jacob, Balthasar's father, who was born in 1594, and Balthasar's mother Ursula Hirschmann.

Bopfingen is first identified in German records around AD 775. It is overlooked by the 700-metre Ipf mountain, whose flattened summit gives it the look of a table. It is this main feature that is as familiar to today's visitor as it would have been to the Mocks. The vineyards then, as now, produced some of the world's best wine, including the famous Riesling. Bopfingen today remains small and agriculture-based, with white-walled, orange-roofed houses, some of which may well originate from the sixteenth and seventeenth centuries. It is peaceful, calm and friendly, and betrays little evidence of a bloody history.

But when Jacob and Ursula married in 1632, a war like nothing ever experienced, a killing machine on a scale reminiscent of the plague that decimated the whole of the known world in the fourteenth century, had been ravaging the region for nearly fifteen years. The Thirty Years War, which ran from 1618 to 1648, engulfed all of continental western Europe. It is believed to have taken the lives of 20 per cent of the population. But it was much worse than that in Baden-Württemberg, where fully three quarters of the Mocks' friends, neighbours and relatives were killed in the fighting or as a result of the famine and disease the conflict wrought. (Almost nothing that was good came out of the Thirty Years War, but one thing that did was the legacy of Vincent de Paul, a French priest whose charitable endeavours in the first fifty years of the seventeenth century, some people think, marked the birth of what we today call humanitarian work. The Society of St Vincent de Paul, later founded in his name, now works in 153 countries. The England and Wales branch was established in 1844, and Patrick Connolly, your great-grandfather, was a committed member and volunteer, doing good works often with the assistance of his daughter Stella.)

The war continued to rage for three more years after Balthasar was born in Bopfingen in 1645. It had blighted and overshadowed Jacob and Ursula's lives. But they clearly had something about them, for they not only survived but, presumably eager to avoid Balthasar's life experience mirroring their own, were somehow able to set their son on a path down which no-one in the family had ever ventured. Ursula seems to have been a miracle-worker, because the records tell us that she was already fifty when Balthasar was born. She died when he was eleven, but perhaps it was she, in the few years they had together, who instilled in him the desire to find something better.

We can only speculate about the path that Balthasar took. Resolving to leave was probably the easy part. How to do so would have required a bit more thought. But there were not many options. Most people then went everywhere – which was hardly anywhere, and nowhere far away – on their own two legs. The lucky few might have had a horse, which then turned out not to be so lucky because they were almost inevitably dragooned into the military campaign and were unlikely to last long after that. More extended travel was via the waterways. One possibility open to Balthasar was to head towards the Danube, and journey south and east. Another option was the River Neckar, close to home and navigable, and which joins the Rhine and then flows a thousand kilometres – a journey then of several weeks – to the North Sea. The Danube, Neckar, Rhine and other major rivers, then, as subsequently, were huge commercial thoroughfares, with a constant procession of boats in both directions carrying everything and everyone.

How would Balthasar have made a choice? Well, he may not have had one, nor much useful information to base one on, but had he been in the position to choose his next steps, the Neckar and the Rhine would have looked the best bet. The people of Baden-Württemberg were Protestants. The war was, partly at least, about religion. Even by the early 1660s, when Balthasar was probably on the move, heading in the Catholic direction – in other words to France or Spain, or east or south towards what is today Bavaria and onwards to Austria or Italy – was unlikely to appeal. That said, some of the north and westerly options can't have looked very attractive either. Take England for example. The English were in the midst of their own civil war the year Balthasar was born. Less than four years later, they would execute their king, Charles I, beheading him in January 1649. Chaos reigned, and no-one knew how it would end. Probably not the place to go if you were aiming for a more peaceful, settled life.

I'm guessing that Balthasar decided (if he had a choice, as opposed to simply becoming a victim of circumstance or other people's decisions, which would have been the case if his way out was to work a passage with some trader or other traveller) just to follow the flow of the rivers north and see what transpired. If that's what happened, he would in all likelihood ultimately have found himself in Rotterdam, where the Rhine flows into the North Sea. And there the choices would perhaps have opened up again. The talk of the town in Rotterdam in the early 1660s may still have been the hullabaloo around Charles II, the king of England who launched his journey back there to assume the throne in 1660. There is a famous painting in the Rijksmuseum in Amsterdam of Charles setting off with his ships; it was clearly an event of some notoriety.

Charles intended to reclaim the kingdom following the death of Oliver Cromwell, who had been responsible for beheading Charles' father and abolishing the monarchy before establishing himself as, to all intents and purposes, dictator of the British Isles. (He preferred the title Lord Protector, but no-one was fooled by that.) Balthasar may easily have heard about all this, and it's hard to imagine that heading to England would have seemed the obvious choice for someone aiming for a quieter, safer and better existence than the one he had just escaped. A more exotic option would have been the Dutch East Indies, mostly in and around what today is Indonesia, and Rotterdam was the stepping-off point for that too. However, the East Indies was really an adventure for professional sailors and traders hoping to make a fortune and then return home to enjoy it, and not so much for someone from Europe looking to start a new life with people like themselves.

The place many Protestants from Europe were actually choosing to emigrate to at that time was the New World of the Americas. From before the 1650s, there was a burgeoning traffic to the so-called New Netherlands, stretching from Delaware up to Rhode Island and to the west of what became Cape Cod. We can imagine that Balthasar, a young, single man in what then passed for the prime of life, and therefore an attractive recruit for either settlers wishing to plump up their numbers or a ship's captain looking for crew, fell into conversation and learned of a ship heading for somewhere called Barnstable on the south of Cape Cod. Probably he had never previously heard of either of those places, but they could still have sounded like the answer to his problem.

It was, admittedly, quite a risk. The ships undertaking the transatlantic voyage were poorly built, crowded, disease-ridden and very short on food. Worse, the journey took an age: it could be six weeks, but it could also be as long as three months, all depending on the wind, the weather and whether the captain and crew had any idea what they were doing. Most of them didn't, not least because this was the era before people had the tools and knowledge to navigate with any accuracy on the open sea. So exactly where you would end up was also in the lap of the gods. No doubt it all looked very cheerful and optimistic sailing off into the sunset for the first few hours or even days. The captains and those selling passages were unlikely to have told the full truth about how gruelling the journey would be – if they even knew. While Balthasar could not have known quite how dangerous and unpredictable the venture was, it cannot have been beyond him to realise he was taking a big chance. Many people died, and many others barely survived the hunger, boredom and sea sickness of the transatlantic voyage, to say nothing of the threats from their unruly fellow passengers and crew. On some of the Atlantic crossings around that time, fewer than half survived the voyage and then the initial, often terrifyingly cold, winter months in the New World.

Imagine Balthasar's feelings, then, when not three months after embarking, but just a matter of days after waving goodbye to Rotterdam, his ship found land-fall in a small but well-developed port populated with fishing vessels, and attractively backed by gently rolling green hills woven with lanes bordered by ancient hedgerows. I've had more than enough of this boat, he may have thought. But is this Barnstable, he could have asked. Yes, this is Barnstaple, would have come the reply. Language difficulties would have added to the confusion. It's hard to believe Balthasar was much of an English speaker, or that there were many German speakers on the north Devon coast. But, while Barnstaple may not have been Barnstable, it was at least safe land. In fact, the latter town had taken its name from the former one: perhaps Balthasar concluded fate was giving him a strong hint.

In other words, Balthasar may have been aiming to get to Barnstable in Cape Cod in the New World of the Americas, and by accident found himself instead in Barnstaple in Devon. Perhaps his original plan was to recuperate for a while in Barnstaple and then resume the journey. But then he met Marrian Passmore, a teenager from the village of Landkey, just a short walk from Barnstaple. They married in 1665. And that was that.

Within a year of marrying, in 1666 Balthasar and Marrian had a son, John. Six subsequent generations lived their lives within just a few miles of Barnstaple. Many of their births were registered in the church at Georgeham, which is part of the parish of Braunton; there were several members of the family who were buried there too, and whose gravestones (and therefore presumably whose remains) are still there. The record keepers of the Anglican church of Georgeham did an unusually good job for more than 200 years, which is why we have been able to track down your ancestors.

At roughly the same time as Balthasar Mock was born in Bopfingen, John Lowcocke was born in Skipton in Yorkshire. Together with an unknown woman, he had a son, George Lowcock, in 1684. George distinguished himself by marrying a woman of exceptional longevity, Jane Carr, who appeared in 1682 and apparently lasted exactly a hundred years, to 1782. George himself did not do badly for the time, but he only lived half as long as his wife, dying in 1734. John Lowcocke was the first of six generations of Lowcocks we have identified from Skipton.

Positioned thirty miles north-west of Leeds on the River Aire, at the entrance to the Yorkshire Dales, Skipton is now a market town with a population of about 15,000. It is regularly lauded by *The Sunday Times* as among the best places to live in Britain. Its origins go back a long way, as do probably the Lowcock family's with it. The town was listed in the Domesday Book of 1086. One Robert de Romille, a Norman baron who was part of William the Conqueror's entourage, established Skipton Castle from 1090, and the castle proved the focal point and protective hub for the community that developed over the following centuries. The main thing you may want to know about Skipton, though, is that it was all about sheep. Indeed, the name means "Sheep Town", with the local economy and most people's livelihoods for seven hundred years after the castle was established all based on sheep: breeding them, looking after them, shearing them, spinning the thread, weaving the cloth, killing them and marketing the meat. In all probability it was sheep – and not much else – that helped the Lowcocks of Skipton make ends meet for hundreds of years.

So now we have met those among the first and second generations of our ten-generation family story. As we shall see later, however, other branches of the family were likely making their way in various parts of Ireland, in and around Liverpool, in the Lake District and the north-east of England, in north Wales, in Sweden and in northern Germany and/or the Baltic countries. What was life actually like for all of them and the Mocks and the Lowcocks in the sixteenth and seventeenth centuries?

We don't know what they looked like, sounded like, said, thought, enjoyed, feared or believed. There are no pictures. In the days before photography only the super-rich, and hardly any of them, were recorded by portrait painters. There are no sound records of anyone before the nineteenth century. We don't know if any of your sixteenth-

and seventeenth-century forebears could read and write –
quite likely not – and there are no diary or other records of
their thoughts or feelings. We don't how they spent their
days or how they made a living. We can, though, make
a few educated guesses based on what is known about
people like them.

While the better off might have had brick-or stone-
built houses, the poorer sorts like the Lowcocks and the
Mocks, especially in rural areas, mostly lived in small
timber-framed cottages, with wickerwork and plaster walls,
and thatched roofs (which needed replacing periodically,
though the raw material was always available). The basic
structure was quite durable. In the 1980s my brother Nick
and I lived in just this sort of house in Hertfordshire, and
it had originally been built in the sixteenth century. There
are still some of these houses left in Braunton, which
could conceivably have once housed Balthasar Mock and
his heirs. When built, these houses had a minimal number
of windows, because windows were one of the few things
that were taxed. There was no running water, heating or
lighting. There was sometimes some sort of cess pit, a mixed
blessing at best because they stank and often overflowed.
The nearest tree, bush or field was often a better bet for
bodily functions. Many people shared their living space
with their animals, both for warmth and for safeguarding
the livestock. The olfactory implications of that are not to
be sniffed at.

This was one of the coldest recorded periods, called in
fact a Little Ice Age, and few people could afford enough
coal or wood for fires to keep warm. Some burned peat. But
many simply shivered. People had a handful of belongings
– maybe sticks of furniture, wooden plates, earthenware
for beer, a knife to eat with (forks being the preserve of

the better off) and a few clothes. Men wore knee-length breeches, the predecessor to trousers, with stockings and boots, linen shirts and waistcoats and jackets. The cloth they were made from was typically scratchy and uncomfortable. Women wore long nightdress-like garments called shifts. Over the shifts they wore dresses, made up of bodices and skirts; under them there was nothing. Underwear was not in fashion.

Life was short. Most people died before they were thirty. The first preoccupation for all bar maybe the richest 10 per cent of the population was getting enough food to survive. Famine had struck in living memory, for example in Cumberland and Westmorland in the 1620s. Many people were hungry from one day to the next, month after month and year after year. For the large majority, the stock diet, without variation except during the fruit and vegetable harvesting seasons, was bread (especially in the south), potatoes and oatcakes (further north). Anything you've read of roast beef and sumptuous feasts certainly did not play much part in your ancestors' experience. Everyone drank beer – an average of more than a hundred gallons a year each, so two or three pints a day, every day. Beer in fact was the main and often only thing many people had for breakfast. Most of it was brewed very locally, by innkeepers and taverns. On average, there was a pub for every 300 people across the country. That created lots of employment opportunities, of course, and we shall meet some of your ancestors who were innkeepers and barmen.

People spent most of the daylight hours outdoors and working: planting, ploughing, harvesting, fruit picking, shepherding, lambing and shearing, and then for some at home in the cottage, spinning, weaving, making clothes or lace, and tanning animal skins (hence the phrase cottage industry). The outdoor life was brutally exhausting and draining, especially for the poorly nourished, and from a young age all were debilitated by rheumatism, rickets, scurvy, arthritis, bruises, aches and pains. Most men and women were hunched up and broken bodied by the time they reached their forties.

Of course there were no medical services worth the name: no painkillers (except in so far as alcohol helped, and opioids for the very small minority who could afford them), no anaesthetics – and as a result very little surgery – and no antibiotics. So if, as happened to the population of London in the year Balthasar and Marrian married, you were caught up in an outbreak of the plague, it was likely to be deadly: estimates suggest that 20 per cent of the capital's population died in that year alone. The fleas and lice that carried the disease were everywhere, and people were constantly preoccupied by scratching and fighting them off. Hygiene was rudimentary at best. Most people washed their hands, wrists, faces and neck – the parts that could be seen – in cold water every morning. But baths for the sake of keeping clean were rare, partly because of the danger of picking up an infection from the dirty water.

An even bigger killer than the plague was tuberculosis, made worse by the fact that no-one knew it was infectious, so when it passed from one family member sharing cramped accommodation to another, the assumption was simply that there was an inherited weakness. Dental problems too contributed a surprising amount to early death. Tooth rot was widespread, and when excruciating pain indicated an infection, the choice was ominous: the huge agony of having the tooth ripped out by the nearest person with pliers, frequently the blacksmith, or the risk of a slower but also painful death from the infection. Half the population faced another major killer: childbirth. Natural labour was the only option. In the absence of anaesthetics, caesarean births were almost unheard of, and there is no record of a mother surviving one in Britain before the 1790s (when there were still no anaesthetics). Unsurprisingly, labour took the lives of one woman in twenty-five, and one in ten of those who had six or more children, as many did.

It must have been tempting to turn to religion in the hope of some protection from all this. Dread of disease, both actual and potential, and fear of mortality, together with the total absence of any useful medical services to combat them, provide an excellent rationale for prayer. Maybe 90 per cent of the population belonged to the Church of England (though it was different in Ireland, as we shall see). Religious persecution was dying out across England by the late seventeenth century, but the vast majority of people associated themselves with the Anglican Church and various other Protestant spin-offs. King James II, the monarch at the end of the seventeenth century, was a Catholic and as such was accepted only with misgivings. Religious belief also sat alongside all sorts of other weird superstitions and myths. In 1682, as Balthasar and Marrian were bringing up their family just a few miles down the road, three old women were accused of witchcraft in Bideford. They were subject to a series of ludicrous interrogations, examinations and tests – including, for example, to establish whether they could travel invisibly, to try to demonstrate that their bodies had been marked with deformities by the devil and in an attempt to throw light on whether they had caused shipwrecks by talking about them. The local mayor decided they were guilty. They were sent to Exeter, and the judge there seems to have decided he couldn't overturn the ruling, so they were hanged.

Social, family and state violence was widespread. Women at home were particularly vulnerable. Husbands, fathers and employers were allowed to beat them at will with no-one batting an eyelid, provided no-one actually died. Following the havoc and destruction of the civil war in the middle of the seventeenth century, there was a period of greater stability. England was internally relatively peaceful from the eras of Balthasar Mock and John Lowcocke onwards, though the country did join in European and wider wars throughout the eighteenth and nineteenth centuries.

People's rights were restricted. While Parliament functioned and there were elections, only one adult in eight, and none of the women, had the vote. I doubt any of your ancestors were among them. That is not to say that everyone spent all day touching their forelocks and curtseying to the gentry. There were basic rights, but they were limited. There were some modest economic protections. The 1601 Poor Law established a responsibility for each parish – the main local unit of organisation – to appoint overseers of the poor, who could gather taxes to provide for those who could not work, including the old and disabled. (Those who could work but refused were whipped and put in houses of correction.) Such paupers – people supported by the parish – had to wear a blue or red "P" on their clothes. Their children were sent to local employers to be apprentices. But this system did mean that in an era when harvests – and so the weather – determined everything, bad years, in England at least, did not by this time produce famines, unlike across much of the rest of Europe. Despite the Poor Law, the tax system in the seventeenth century was regressive. Most tax was raised on things consumed by the poor, like salt. The richest were protected, because there were no taxes on income or land.

The total population of England and Wales was only five million, and the vast majority – including all of your ancestors we have found – lived in the countryside. The country was quite empty and disconnected: a myriad of small, insular communities. Most people never ranged far from the place where they were born. These rural dwellers correspondingly met few other people. And the ones they did meet tended to be exactly like them – with the same life experiences, beliefs, knowledge and indeed relatives. On one level that made for predictability, because you were unlikely to be surprised by other people. On the other hand, it made for a restricted and narrow experience. And if you did meet someone different – a traveller from elsewhere, for example – curiosity and interest were quite likely to be overwhelmed by fear of the unknown. That is one of the things that makes Balthasar's relationship with Marrian so intriguing.

What about fun? Festivals were popular. Alcohol. Smoking tobacco in pipes was very common. Singing. Cards and various ball games. Most people kept daylight hours. Only the well-off could afford candles or lanterns, the main form of light after dark. So to the extent people did have any fun in the non-working hours, it was mostly of the sort that you can do in the dark. And that kind of thing was, by the way, just as much enjoyed by your ancestors as it is today. Maybe even more so, given the lack of alternatives.

Back in Devon, Balthasar Mock's son John married Prudence Calverley in Braunton in September 1690. She had been born there in 1670. He was twenty-four and she was twenty. So they were both four years younger than the average age for men and women at marriage. Since people generally married only when they were able to afford to set up home for themselves, he must have had a reasonably secure income. Prudence seems to have lived her whole life in Braunton, and she died there too, in 1758, twenty-two years after her husband. In 1692 John and Prudence had a son. They christened him Balthasar after his noteworthy grandfather. Whether the elder Balthasar was aware of that is unclear. There is no trace of him after his marriage in 1665.

2

Better Rags:
The Eighteenth Century

*in which four generations of Mocks stayed exactly
where Balthasar and Marrian had started in
Devon, four generations of Lowcocks did the
same in Skipton, and we meet the Watsons and
Gillbankses in the Lake District.*

I n this chapter we primarily cover the third, fourth and
(parts of the) fifth generations of the family – though
some of the second generation also saw the start of
the eighteenth century, and a few of the sixth generation
saw its end. The eighteenth century was a broadly peaceful
era at home in Britain. The population grew from about
5 million in 1700 to 8.6 million in 1800. In 1700 three
quarters of the population were rural: small-scale farmers,
labourers or cottagers and paupers. A century later, more
were moving to towns and cities – though none of your
ancestors had yet done that.

The standard of living for most people was notably
higher by the end than at the beginning of the century.
And there was a north and west versus south and east

divide: in 1700 wages were about 60 per cent higher in London than in the West Country. Pandemics – typhoid and other diseases – meant the population fell in the 1720s and 1730s before recovering. It would have cost around £30 –40 a year to support a family. But rock-bottom agricultural wages were, at about a shilling (5p) a day, a lot lower than that, meaning that many people were constantly on the verge of starvation. At the beginning of the century two loaves of bread would have cost about a shilling. You could also have got twelve beers for a shilling, and that would have nourished you for the day, though you might not have earned much during it – or been in much of a state to do so the following day. Had you enough money, and I don't think the Mocks or the Lowcocks did, you could have got a newly built two-up, two-down brick cottage for £150.

The last quarter of the century was increasingly volatile, in all sorts of ways. Population growth accelerated. Bread prices quadrupled. The major colony, America, was lost to independence. But better roads and canals were starting to cut transport times and costs. That, and the arrival of newspapers and growing literacy, meant information spread further and faster. Innovation and technology were making agriculture more productive, which made it possible for more people to move to the towns and cities. Trade – cotton, coal, sugar and slaves – was bringing people into the ports, including Liverpool, to where many of your forebears would gravitate.

Devon at the beginning of the eighteenth century was a more important part of the country than it is now. The population in 1700 was around 350,000, meaning one Briton in fourteen was from there. Now it is closer to one in eighty. In Barnstaple, the nearest significant town to the Mocks, the port silted up around this time, putting a significant dampener on local prosperity. Fishermen in other Devon ports were making a mint feeding the growing London population. The Devon woollen industry was in decline through this period too, out-competed by Yorkshire and Lancashire. The modest village of Georgeham and the slightly larger one of Braunton each amounted to no more than several hundred people, most of whom knew each other throughout their lives. In Georgeham they showed up together at the church, where many of the Mocks are buried. They got their beer from the same inns – The King's Arms and The Rock, both of which are still there.

When we left them in 1692, John and Prudence Mock had just christened their baby son Balthasar. This Balthasar eventually married Esther Garnis, also of Braunton, in 1717. She was twenty-two. But, like a great many of her contemporaries, she was not to be blessed with a long life, moving on in 1735 before she reached her fortieth birthday. She did, though, bring forth a son, another John, in 1718, just a year after she married. That John, one of many John Mocks in the line – innovation in family names not being something the Mocks went in for much – married Margaret Purser in 1750. They too had a son, also John, in March 1753. That sequence of three generations of Mock men, Balthasar, John and John, enjoyed unusual longevity, living to the ages of 85, 78 and 66 respectively. In 1776 the latter John married Mary Wyburn, who you will by now be unsurprised to learn was also from Braunton, having been born there in 1755. So through the whole of the eighteenth century, the Mock men stuck close to home and married local women.

And three hundred miles to the north, four generations of Lowcock men did just the same. George and Jane Lowcock's son, also George, was born in Skipton in

1708. He married Ellenor Atkinson, and the two of them produced another son, William, in 1742. William married Susannah Hartley and duly became father in 1767 to John Lowcock. And it was that John Lowcock – who like his forebears had been born, lived and died in Skipton – who, having married Mary Clegg, fathered the John Lowcock who would finally move the family beyond Skipton.

By definition, those of your direct ancestors we have identified lived full adult lives and had their own families and children. It is worth noting, though, that many of their brothers and sisters did not. One child in five did not survive their first year; one in three never made it past their fifth birthday; and a staggering three London children in four in the 1740s died before they were six years old. And the Grim Reaper harvested the poorest. Poverty and the absence of any useful medical services pervasively resulted in early death. But this was also a violent era: every child was hit at home, and at school if they went there, which the majority still did not. Child labour was universal, there was constant street fighting, criminals were publicly whipped and pilloried, and people sometimes fought and drank themselves to death in escapades that started out as fun and got out of control. The worst criminals were hanged and, by the end of the century, deported to Australia. Though the death penalty was rare, around a couple of hundred people a year were still hanged. None of your ancestors were among them. Some of them were criminals though, as we shall see when we move on to the nineteenth century.

You will have noticed that very little of what we have said so far comes from the female perspective. Women were the majority of the population in the eighteenth century, just as they are now. They carried out pretty much all the hard work men did – in the fields, workshops, domestic service, taverns and elsewhere, though fewer of the violent jobs (including fighting wars). But they were paid only two thirds of what men received. Women were subjugated and subordinated in almost every way. They had no rights over their children or matrimonial property. Nothing was theirs: on marriage or death everything went to husbands or male heirs. Avoiding marriage, by the way, didn't help. Spinsterhood was no protection from predatory male relatives. Formally speaking, marriage therefore effectively reduced women to the status of drudges and chattels.

Up to the beginning of the seventeenth century, marriage was frequently an economic bargain or necessity, with the choice often largely imposed on ordinary women. By 1800, while nothing had changed legally, women seem increasingly to have acquired more say over who they would marry, and personal choice and even love became relevant criteria for more of them in picking a husband.

What seventeenth- and eighteenth-century women thought about all this is almost entirely a matter of conjecture. Most of what is known about ordinary women from that time comes from records left not by them but by men. Jane Austen, whose novels were largely written early in the nineteenth century but reflected her early life late in the eighteenth century, started to redress that through her depiction of her female characters.

In practice, many women may have had more power and influence day to day than their formal status implies. Many marriages were mutually beneficial household partnerships, suiting both sides. Women gained a degree of independence as producers and proprietors and some status and protection against other men from their husbands. They frequently outlived their husbands and widows inherited businesses. Marriage was often quickly followed by – and sometimes, including for several of your forebears, prompted by – pregnancy. Across the country as a whole, falling marriage ages from the end of the eighteenth century and the early nineteenth century was one of the drivers of the rapid growth of the population. Changing childcare practices was another, with, for example, more cuddling and cradling of young babies seemingly contributing to lower infant mortality as time passed.

Teenagers from the social strata of your forebears were often sent into service, becoming servants in the houses of the better-off farmers or tradespeople, or the gentry and aristocracy. Many boys also took up apprenticeships, which could be for seven years, to learn a trade. Only once they had established themselves did they tend to marry. For one thing, they needed enough money to be able to set up house, which is what the newly married typically did, rather than staying in one or other of the parental homes. The eighteenth-century Balthasar, John and John Mock, like their contemporaries George, William and John Lowcock, generally did not marry until they reached their mid-twenties – in some cases later – and one effect of that was to contain family size and therefore population growth. As later generations married a bit earlier, so family size, and the population as a whole, grew.

What did your eighteenth-century forebears think about their lives? One obvious point is that, hard as their lives may look to us, they had nothing to compare them to. Eighteenth-century society was highly differentiated. The gulfs between the rich and the poor, the rulers (hardly any of them) and the ruled (statistically, pretty much everyone) were huge, much bigger than today's inequalities. Class and economic hierarchies dominated life. Everyone was expected to know their place and stick to it. Some writers would have us believe that the poorer sorts actually liked that, because it at least made for a predictable situation. Everyone knew where they stood, however bad a place it was.

Joseph Watson, born around 1765, was an innkeeper from Hesket-in-the-Forest. Hesket is an ancient parish north of the Lake District, halfway between Penrith and Carlisle and just off what is today the M6 motorway. The parish embraces what in the Middle Ages were called the townships of High and Low Hesket. And, as the name implies, it covers the core of the royal forest of Inglewood, across the lowland areas west of the River Eden. The forest, used for hunting parties, had been held by the Crown since the time of King Richard III in the early 1480s. In 1696 the then king, William III, gave it to William Bentinck, Duke of Portland, and it passed subsequently between various other aristocratic families. But over time, the forest was increasingly cleared to make way for agriculture, which, with fisheries – the Eden was a rich fishing resource – provided almost everyone's living.

Being an innkeeper like Joseph may have been preferable to scraping a living off the soil. A lot of the work was indoors out of the weather for one thing, which must always have been an advantage in the cold, wet and windy Lake District. That said, being an innkeeper was statistically among the deadliest of jobs, presumably because it frequently put you in the midst of drunken violence breaking out among your patrons. Joseph may have gone to school – one was endowed in Hesket in 1763, two years before he was born – and perhaps he could read and write. The approach to education of that era was instrumental – in other words, you were more likely to be literate and numerate if you needed to be in order to make a living. Innkeepers, with books to balance and money to count, may well have been in that category. Joseph married Mary Thompson, four years his younger, and in 1793 they had a son, Edward, also born in Hesket.

While your Watson ancestors were wending their way through the eighteenth century in Hesket, your Gillbanks forebears were doing much the same twelve miles further north. They were in Threlkeld, a tiny village just outside Keswick, the prominent Lake District town. The first of them we have found was William Gillbanks, who was born in August 1704. Threlkeld sits in a lush green valley surrounded by fells. Evidence of human activity in the valley goes back at least five thousand years. Originally forested – like so much of the country – the woodlands were gradually cleared and some two thousand years ago scattered communities began to appear. Early remains of buildings estimated to be from between AD 300 and 900 are still in evidence in Threlkeld. A thousand years later, when we find the Gillbanks family, agriculture was the base of the economy. The climate facilitates farming – warmer, dryer and sunnier in the summer, making the harvest easier, but enough rain year round to allow crops to ripen in the valley and to keep the grassland green and rich for the cattle.

William Gillbanks married Mary Cockbain, two or three years older than him, and in July 1741 their son George was born, also in Threlkeld. George Gillbanks himself had a son, Abraham, born in 1762 once more in Threlkeld. Abraham married Nancy Heskett, from Allonby, a village on the Cumbrian coast north of Workington. On today's roads it is twenty-six miles from Allonby to Threlkeld. That was a vast distance for most people when Abraham and Nancy were alive. We can only speculate about what brought them together. But it is worth bearing in mind that many men from Threlkeld, tiny as it was, would have had to look further afield than the village for a wife unless they were ready to marry their sister, which generally they weren't, and which was anyway frowned upon. We do know that Nancy and Abraham made Threlkeld home. In 1793, when Nancy was twenty-three, their son William Gillbanks was born there. Abraham reached the premier league for longevity among your ancestors, surviving to the age of ninety-five before finally passing on in 1857.

The Lowcocks, Watsons, Gillbankses and Mocks of the eighteenth century, from whom you are descended, were probably not at the very bottom of the economic and social pile, but they would not have been that far up it either. (Their Welsh and Irish counterparts of that time were probably living even harsher lives.) The Watsons and the Gillbankses may have been a little better positioned than the Mocks and Lowcocks: in the Lake District at that time, owner-occupying small-scale farmers were the largest group, and they were materially advantaged over the wage labouring classes and paupers. But this is a guess based on averages across the society as a whole, and we don't know enough about the actual position of any of the individual people we have identified to be sure.

Why was it that people were so likely never to move beyond where they were born? Part of it was purely practical. Most roads up to the eighteenth century were absolutely dire: seas of mud, ruts and rocks. The road journey from London to Edinburgh could take a fortnight. (Not, by the way, that eighteenth-century people always did that journey by road – it was often quicker and sometimes safer by sea.) Another factor was fear of the unknown. Highwaymen and robbers were a real problem and they deterred unnecessary adventure, even if in practice robbery and murder were less likely on the roads than the popular imagination may have held. In addition to the logistical constraints, there were also rules that prevented mobility. Ordinary people were in principle required to obtain a certificate of permission to move, even to get a new job, though in good times that was sometimes waived.

Things began to ease up somewhat by the end of the century. Roads were improved, though the coaches on them and the horses that pulled them remained much the same. Journey times from London to Manchester fell from ninety hours at the start of the eighteenth century to thirty-three at the end; and from London to Bath from fifty to sixteen. That was purely a result of better road construction and maintenance, often directly financed by road users through tolls. The developing economy was starting to pull more workers into towns and cities from the rural areas. We will shortly see what that meant for some of our characters – and also how others of them were not affected at all.

Less of the improvement in life likely enjoyed by successive generations of Gillbankses, Mocks, Lowcocks and Watsons was experienced in Ireland. It remained the most colonised part of Britain, a Catholic population bullied and bled by frequently absent Protestant landlords, who sent much of the rent they collected back to England. Ireland, unlike England, accordingly suffered famines in the 1720s and 1730s, but the population continued to grow throughout the century, at an even faster rate than in England. That was to have ominous consequences in the following era, as will shortly be revealed.

But in England, the eighteenth century was an era of quiet improvement for most people, albeit with bumpy periods as in the 1730s and 1740s and the last years of the century. While the "average" family were buying £10 a year of British-made goods in the 1680s, that had risen to £25 by 1750 and £40 by 1810. For most people, including those of the position and status of your ancestors, life remained gruelling, with pain exceeding pleasure and what looks to us to be oppressive social structures and huge inequality. By the nineteenth century that was attracting a political reaction from many. But in the eighteenth century it was possible for writers like Samuel Johnson to say, "mankind are happier in a state of inequality and subordination" without attracting widespread ridicule.

Education levels were gradually improving, with the help of schools like the one that appeared in Hesket in 1763. Schools were typically funded through the Church or philanthropy. And newspapers and magazines started to appear all over the country by the end of the century. Yet most people remained functionally illiterate and many could not even write their names on the wedding register, scratching a mark instead. On the other hand, most jobs did not require literacy, so the incentive to acquire it was limited. Children learned songs and nursery rhymes, many of them still passed down the generations into the later twentieth century, which were intended among other things to promote desired behaviours and conformity. People were becoming materially better off: workers possessed beds, sheets, blankets, pots, pans and probably a few pieces of furniture. Until the last years of the century, when a spike in food prices brought renewed problems, few people were verging on starvation or complete hopelessness.

There were lots of good reasons to conform and not rock the boat. The family was the key institution. The most common form of household was one couple with their pre-teen children. Teenagers were typically apprenticed off – including in the case of girls into domestic service – and lived with their employers. New households were formed when couples married – and the timing of that depended mostly on when they could afford to set themselves up, though in some cases pregnancy forced marriage and therefore household establishment. Dutiful sons would inherit, while runaways would not. Despite the inequality, women were generally better off in marriages, and in avoiding having children before marriage. (Though it was often a close-run thing: a notable number of your forebears married and had their first child the same year.) Most marriages ended in death.

Navigating all this was often difficult for adolescent girls and young women. Many were sent as teenagers into domestic service where they were vulnerable to sexual exploitation, from which, given the prevailing power balances, the general acceptability of harassment and the almost complete absence of means of contraception, they had little but their wits to protect them. However big the temptation, the imperative of avoiding pregnancy, which required dodging sexual advances, would have cooled female ardour. Early pregnancy to unmarry-able men was disastrous for young women's life chances, and they all knew it. Nevertheless, there appears to have been an increase in children being born out of wedlock during the course of the eighteenth century.

People worked from cradle to grave: children looked after animals, helped with the washing and did other chores, beginning from around the age they learned to walk. Only infirmity brought an end to work at the other end of life. Medicine remained dire, with doctors very frequently doing more harm than good, and inflicting extreme pain even when they did do something that helped. Very few people in fact ever saw a doctor. This was no loss, because the most that even the best of them could offer was a listening ear, care and compassion. The vast majority were bogus quacks, like James Graham, an eighteenth-century Scot who told his patients that mud baths were the remedy for their ailments, Joshua Ward who made a fortune selling his home-made pill (also available in drop form), including to gullible members of the royal family, and James Morison who got rich on his bogus vegetable pills. (This is not just an eighteenth-century phenomenon: at the turn of the twenty-first century, Americans were visiting providers of unconventional therapies like homeopathy more often than they were going to their family doctors.) The end of the eighteenth century did however see the first occurrences of immunisation, with smallpox inoculation successfully developed and used by Edward Jenner. Hospitals also began to spring up in more places across the country. Fortunately, for the most part they focused on care and convalescence rather than treatment. And there was one noteworthy innovation in maternal care, with the invention of medical forceps in the 1730s, and books containing diagrams showing how to use them by the 1790s.

What about rest, relaxation and fun? Sunday was a day of enforced inactivity. (As it remained long into the future, right up to the twentieth century: no shops, theatres, cinemas, sports events, etc did business on Sundays until quite recently.) That did not mean everyone flocked to church: many people in fact rarely went between the events of baptism and burial, except for weddings. Festivals accompanied by fairs were one of the best opportunities for fun: food, drink, gambling, dancing, music and sport. Music, or at least singing, happened at work too, with teams of agricultural labourers singing songs or shanties to relieve the boredom or add energy to their work. Haircuts at the time of the full moon were a thing, as was bloodletting on your birthday. Cutting a vein with a blade and releasing the blood every now and then was thought to be good for you. The seaside holiday was invented around this time, if only for the well-off, and was championed in Brighton by the royal family.

Diet remained monotonous and meagre for the masses, bread and cheese predominating. Poor-quality tea, with the leaves used multiple times, was to some degree replacing milk and beer. Coffee and sugar were spreading too. Most people saw little improvement in their living accommodation. While there was a gradual growth in the proportion of people who lived in brick-built houses, for the most part dwellings were much the same as they had always been. So, still no indoor plumbing – never mind heating, except open fires – or electricity. There was however the beginning of a gradually growing interest in cleanliness, in large part arising from the desire of the servant-hiring classes to be waited on by people who were less dirty and less smelly.

The average age at death gradually increased from twenty-five or thirty during the sixteenth century to at least the forties two hundred years later. Less tangibly, there is also a sense that Britain at the end of the eighteenth century was, in terms of how people thought of and behaved towards each other, in some ways a somewhat kinder, gentler place than it had been a hundred years earlier. Adults seem to have become more attentive to their children's feelings, cuteness and wishes. Flogging and beating eased off a tad, and was occasionally replaced with reason, kindness, hugging and encouragement. But these were small changes, and not uniform. By any standards that we would recognise, late eighteenth-century life remained nasty, brutal and normally short. Nevertheless, there was optimism about the future. Many people saw opportunities ahead for themselves and their families, and they believed they could navigate hierarchies and expected codes of conduct to their advantage. They thought, in short, that life was going to get better.

3

From Countryside to Cities: The First Half of the Nineteenth Century

---

*in which the Mocks are still in Devon, the
Lowcocks move to Burnley, the Watsons settle in
Watermillock, and we find the first traces of the
McGuinness family in County Cavan, the Lewis
family in Liverpool, the Connollys in Wexford and
the Wilkinsons in Blyth.*

As we saw, life for many of your eighteenth-century predecessors was characterised by slow, gradual but noticeable improvement, in a context of relative national stability. The first decades of the nineteenth century – through which the fifth and sixth generations of the family lived – were more tumultuous. Population growth accelerated, meaning more mouths to be fed in families across the country. Food prices sky-rocketed. An exodus from countryside to town and city gathered pace. The Napoleonic wars, a seismic event across the continent, never saw a shot fired in Britain but large British armies and navies needed raising and paying for. (One thing, by the way, we have yet to find among your ancestors before the twentieth century is any evidence of military service, but it would be surprising if some of them had not chosen or been press-ganged into joining up. One adult man in five in England served in the army or navy during the wars of the early 1800s.)

The historical routines of work around home were permanently disrupted with the huge expansion of factory jobs – including for children – and the coal mining industry. Scientific knowledge, technology and innovation flourished and would later in the century produce a host of products and opportunities improving life dramatically for people of almost every circumstance. But the benefits took time to spread, and the period we are looking at now was chaotic, anarchic, troubled and anxious for many people. The years around 1800 saw a succession of poor harvests, prompting protests and riots. Laws were passed in 1799 and 1800 restricting the formation of groups to campaign for increased wages or political rights. There was a sense of disorder, with illegitimacy, drunkenness and domestic violence all apparently growing. Escape to somewhere better became a theme in several branches of the family, partly because opportunities arose but also because staying put looked, for some at least, like a path to doom.

For some branches of the family, though, the early nineteenth century saw continuity rather than change. When we left them, John Mock and Mary Wyburn, both from Braunton in Devon, had married. They were to live the rest of their lives in Braunton too, as far as we can tell, John dying in 1819. John and Mary did however break with tradition in one respect, by naming the next of your ancestors Job. That may not have been a good idea. Job, born in 1794, in Braunton obviously, turned out to be a problem child. He served a prison sentence in the 1830s, and was tried but this time acquitted of theft in the 1840s. In 1859 a court in Exeter sentenced him to nine months for another felony. After that he was free for a few months, but in May 1861 we find him up for larceny, for which he was imprisoned for twelve months. He did not survive that sentence, dying at Exeter prison in 1862. When not in jail, Job tried to make ends meet as a stonemason, or a builder in modern parlance. Between prison sentences he lived on East Street in Braunton. The road is still there, and many houses from the nineteenth century or earlier have survived. But we are getting a little ahead of ourselves. Job had, in March 1823, married the twenty-two-year-old Elizabeth (Betsy) Richards, who, amazingly, was not from Braunton. Well, it wasn't that amazing. She had been born in Pilton, on the outskirts of Barnstaple. Six miles from Braunton. So they did not have to stretch very far to find each other.

Job and Betsy had had a son, John (reverting to safer name choices, evidently), who was born in 1824. How long Betsy hung around after that is unclear, but she was last recorded at her death in Plato Center, Kane, Illinois in November 1872. How, why and when she went there, we don't know. Maybe she persevered with Job but was so distraught after his death in prison that she needed to start again somewhere completely different. Or maybe she got fed up with him earlier and left.

Meanwhile, the latest John Mock had stuck to what he knew. Live life in Georgeham and Braunton. Marry local girl. Have heirs. Don't move until you die. John married Mary Bennett. They lived at Heanton Street in Braunton, where John, like others in the Mock line, was a stonemason. Their son Edward Mock was born in Georgeham in 1863.

Mary died young, and John subsequently remarried. His new wife was Elizabeth Joslin, seventeen years his junior. So for 200 years Mock men were born in Braunton, married in Braunton, to local girls all from no more than five miles away. They most probably never went further than Barnstaple from the day they were born to the day they died. Edward Mock, though, turned out to be the one to finally break the mould.

John Lowcock, born in Skipton, in North Yorkshire, in 1800, was the latest in the line of Lowcocks of Skipton going back at least 150 years (and probably much longer). John married Elizabeth Malham. She had also been born in Skipton, in 1803. Their son, also John, was born, once again in Skipton, in 1824. But in the 1840s both father and son were to be found in and around Burnley, across the great divide from Yorkshire into Lancashire.

So what changed? It was partly the construction of the Leeds and Liverpool Canal. Travel before the canal age was ruinously expensive for most people, as well as dangerous and difficult, on account of roving brigands and highway robbers. There were few roads, nor many carts or carriages travelling them. The rich, which the Lowcocks never were, had horses and the leisure time and money to ride them. Most people did not. And so they rarely went anywhere further than a day's walk, which, from Skipton, meant essentially nowhere worth going. The canal changed all that (as, to an even greater degree, did the railways that followed soon after). Construction began in 1770, and the full length of the canal was completed in 1822. It ran a total distance of 127 miles, crossing the Pennines. It went through Skipton.

The canal also passed through Burnley. In the medieval period Burnley was a small agricultural community. It

developed by the sixteenth century into a market town
enjoying a large church and a grammar school. By the
eighteenth century, there was a weaving industry, some of
whose raw material may even have come from Skipton.
In the latter half of the eighteenth century, cotton
began gradually to replace wool. That had momentous
implications for the prospects of Skipton (bad) and towns
like Burnley (good, because it was close to a river, which
could provide power for the new spinning machines and
water for cleaning).

John and Elizabeth Lowcock moved with their son John
to Habergham Eaves, just outside Burnley, between 1841
and 1845. They were probably drawn there by the better
jobs offered by the rapidly growing Burnley economy. The
canal, the development of mining on the Burnley coalfield,
and the arrival of newly invented coal-fired steam engines
to provide power to the cotton mills, saw the town take off
in the second quarter of the nineteenth century. By 1866
Burnley was thought to be the largest producer of cotton
cloth in the world. Both the Johns were textile workers (or
tailors, as the family story has it).

The years 1818–20 saw protests in Lancashire against
the introduction of new machinery to do work previously
carried out by people. But the economy picked up, more
jobs were created and the protests died down. New
spinning and weaving technology, and in particular the
expanding cotton industry, were forcing wages in the
wool sector down. Workers reacted to that by protesting
about the technology, including in Luddite riots which
saw new machinery wrecked. This was accompanied by
political reform movements, like the Chartists, who called
for wider voting rights and other reforms. But, not for the
first nor the last time, opposing new technology proved

as successful as pushing water uphill. The Chartists made no progress in terms of their political demands either, though that changed later in the century. In the meantime, Burnley's economic expansion and the new opportunities it created brought in workers, attracted by the higher wages on offer there than elsewhere. The new arrivals included workers like the Lowcocks of Skipton, tempted – or driven by necessity – away from the now declining wool industry in their home town.

While the overall long-term economic trend was upwards, it was concealed by repeated short-term boom and bust. Many of the textile mills closed in 1824, throwing people out of work, when the only bank in the town collapsed. The cotton famine, caused by the American civil war of 1861–65, was equally disastrous. But throughout the nineteenth century, every short-term bust was followed by a better recovery. The railways arrived in Burnley shortly after the Lowcocks, in 1848, linking the population to other places, spreading knowledge and creating yet more new opportunities. The railways also facilitated a whole new leisure experience for the population of the industrialising north-west. They reached Blackpool in the 1840s, setting it on the path to a tourism boom lasting more than a hundred years. Many members of the family have enjoyed the delights of Blackpool, a topic to which we will return.

The younger John Lowcock married the twenty-two-year-old Sarah Winstanley in Burnley in 1845. They stayed in Burnley for just a few years before moving to St Helens, where we will meet them again. They may have been forced to move on by one of the Burnley downturns. And, by the way, they may well have got to St Helens by canal too: first towards Liverpool along the remaining stretch of the great canal from Leeds, and then on the now disused but at the time important Sankey Canal.

The Watson family of Cumberland was not drawn to Lancashire by industrialisation. Edward Watson married Mary Todd (whose family name could easily have been lost on her marriage but was kept running by the Watson family who used it as a middle name for subsequent sons). Mary's parents had got married in 1782 at Watermillock, on Ullswater, deeper into the Lake District. They were probably from there: her mother's maiden name, Mounsey, was later associated with other local features – Mounsey's Boathouse for example. It is quite possible that Edward had gone to Watermillock to take responsibility for the Brackenrigg Inn. His father Joseph had been an innkeeper. It was common for sons to follow the trade of their fathers, partly because the fathers could help them do that. So several of the Mock men in Devon were masons or builders. The Lowcocks included several textile workers, and several branches of the family included successive generations of coal miners. We know that later in the century the Watsons were the keepers of the Brackenrigg Inn, and it is fair to deduce that they probably inherited the tenure from Edward. It's certainly not obvious what else would have brought him to Watermillock from Hesket. And once there he met and married Mary.

Largely because it was subsequently made part of the Lake District National Park, much about Watermillock is pretty much the same now as it was then. It lies nine miles from Penrith, the nearest decent-sized town, on what is now the A592 running along the western side of Ullswater, perhaps the most beautiful of all the lakes in the Lake District. You can see Watermillock, a tiny remote settlement, to your left as you travel up Ullswater on the steamer ferry boat from Glenridding, at the south of the lake, to Howtown on the east side. You get an even better view from the fells above Howtown on the walk back to Glenridding. Behind Watermillock, looking across the water from the Howtown side, you see the remains of the forest, which earlier was good deer hunting ground, and behind them the majestic fells. In the western distance, beyond Glenridding, you can see Helvellyn, arguably England's most impressive mountain.

The Brackenrigg Inn, which was probably the best thing in Watermillock, was used especially by tourists to the Lakes. There was little to draw in the casual or commercial traveller. Tourism began in the late eighteenth century. Previously, this part of the country had been considered remote and foreboding by non-residents. Daniel Defoe, the traveller and author of *Robinson Crusoe*, and a person endowed with a certain spirit of adventure, described the area in 1724 as "the wildest, most barren and frightful of any that I have passed over in England". But by 1820, William Wordsworth, a poet with national reach then (if not so much now, though your grandparents all studied his works at school) published a Lake District guidebook which sold well and brought in lots of visitors. His most famous poem, "Daffodils", which came to be learned by heart by generations of school children, and was better known for its opening line – "I wandered lonely as a cloud" – was about the flowers he saw walking round Ullswater. Wild daffodils were probably a feature there for centuries. Later generations of Watsons gathered them to sell in Penrith.

The early tourists were typically of a prosperous sort, and they weren't coming for the weather. But some of them chose the Lakes ahead of the so-called European

Grand Tour, which wealthy British people liked to do, taking in the great cities of France and Italy. The middle of the nineteenth century saw periods of acute violence and conflict on the continent, and in those years the prosperous British may often have preferred to holiday at home. The railways reached Windermere in 1847. That brought Ullswater and therefore the Brackenrigg Inn into reach for more people.

In 1819 Edward and Mary had a son, another Joseph. He took time to establish himself in a degree of economic security, as many men did in the middle decades of the nineteenth century. He did not marry until he was forty. While the population was increasing rapidly throughout the first half of the century, and the economy was growing and developing, real wages in the rural areas were stagnant. At the same time, food prices were subject to dramatic spikes throughout that period. One result was that many men found they could not afford to marry until later than their fathers' generation had done. That was especially true for those outside the areas in which industrialisation was accelerating. The Lake District was in that category, despite the emergence of a modest coal mining industry.

———·———

We are now moving to Ireland to meet another branch of the family. Ireland was fully incorporated by law into the UK in 1800. The population of Britain (England, Scotland and Wales) was then about ten million. The population of Ireland (then one country) was about five million. So Britain was twice the size of Ireland. Now, the population of Britain is about sixty-four million. And that of the island of Ireland, including Northern Ireland, is about 6.7

million. So Britain used to be twice the size of Ireland, but is now ten times the size. What happened?

It was the Irish potato famine of the 1840s. A million people died. Two million emigrated. For the first forty years of the nineteenth century, the population of Ireland had grown at a similar rate to that of England. It reached eight million by 1840. But there was a crucial difference: Ireland in the 1840s was poorer, more rural and more agricultural. Two thirds of the population were still living off the land. Population growth in England, by contrast, was mostly urban. Only one third of the population were now working in agriculture.

There were other differences too. Male literacy in England was by now around 70 per cent; in Ireland just 50 per cent. Per capita income in Ireland was only 60 per cent of that in England. Many rural people in Ireland lived in one-room huts made from mud. They were desperately poor, many on the knife edge between survival and death. People's rights were also more restricted in Ireland than in England. That was especially true for Catholics – the majority of the population – who had long suffered discrimination. And the electorate, which was still exclusively male and determined mostly on the basis of wealth, was a mere 122,000 in Ireland. Barely more than 1 per cent of the population. In England, it was at least ten times as many.

So Ireland was poorer, more crowded and offered fewer opportunities than England. Most people in Ireland – 55 per cent in the mid-1840s – were entirely dependent for food on the potato. And it was into these circumstances that there arrived the total catastrophe of the potato famine. A fungal disease led to a disastrous crop failure in 1845–46. The yield fell from about eight tons an acre

to about one third of a ton – by more than 95 per cent, in
other words.

Starvation loomed on a vast scale. Many of those who
were able to simply fled. James McGuinness, born in 1823
in Cavanagh, County Cavan, was among them. County
Cavan is now part of the border region joining Ireland
with Northern Ireland. Cavanagh was a tiny place – the
1841 Census of Ireland gives it a population of 74, living in
sixteen houses. James' father, Michael, and mother, Annie,
were both born around 1800. They were Catholics, and
probably from Catholic Irish stock for centuries past.

We know from the church records that James
McGuinness married Susan O'Brien, who was also from
Cavanagh, at St Anthony's Catholic Church in Liverpool
on 22 December 1846. Her father, Michael, and his wife,
also called Susan, were originally from Cavanagh too. And
like so many others they also left Ireland. (In their case,
the destination was Illinois, where Michael died in 1867
followed by his wife Susan in 1869.)

Emigration had in fact started to gather pace in the years
before the famine, with hundreds of thousands leaving before
the failure of the 1845 potato crop. Exactly when James and
Susan left is unclear, but it was certainly before the mass
deaths at the peak of the famine in the years 1847–51. It
took money to escape, as well as wit, and those who left were
by definition able to scrape together the cost of the fare. They
were not the poorest of the poor. Most people, including
those on their way to the US, went first to Liverpool. That
was the route all the main ferryboats took. Liverpool, one
of the world's great trading and passenger ports, could then
connect you with countless other places. For most people,
north America, with its apparently limitless opportunities,
was the destination of choice.

James and Susan must have known each other as children, both being from such a tiny place as Cavanagh. But while her parents found their way to Illinois, James and Susan stayed in Liverpool. Maybe Susan, travelling with her parents, got it together with James on the boat from Ireland, and decided to remain there with him while her parents continued the journey to the US? Many of those, like James and Susan, who ended up staying in Liverpool had originally planned to get to the US, but changed their minds – or ran out of money. Many of the early leavers also subsequently helped other family members to follow them, sending money, offering assistance and reporting back to confirm life was working out better for them. Cavan, where James and Susan had come from, saw a larger exodus than many other counties.

And what was Liverpool – their first and for many their final destination – like by the early nineteenth century? In 1700 it had been a town with a population of less than 10,000. It doubled in size by the middle of the eighteenth century, and reached 70,000 by 1800. That was just the beginning. By the middle of the nineteenth century the population reached 400,000, and Liverpool was the second-largest city in England. So it became forty times as big in 150 years. (It kept growing until the mid-1930s, then the population fell partly as sensitive industries were moved out to protect them from bombardment during the war. After the war, economic decline led to a further exodus, but this was later reversed and by 2011 the population of the city, now revived, had reached a new peak of more than 460,000.)

Liverpool's huge growth was based around the port. The first wet dock in Britain was completed there in 1715, constructed with a capacity of a hundred ships. Britain was

among the first countries to abolish slavery and the slave
trade, early in the nineteenth century. But for the previous
hundred years, 40 per cent of the world's slave activity ran
through ships operating from the docks in Liverpool. This
generated huge profits, which lubricated the expansion of
the city but also helped finance the development of the
textile industry. The port of Liverpool also specialised
in sugar and tobacco, products in high demand among
the rapidly growing British population which had been
enjoying rising incomes through most of the eighteenth
century. Trade also helped Liverpool become one of the
country's leading financial centres.

As well as drawing in immigrants from Ireland,
Liverpool attracted migrants from elsewhere in Britain.
Among them were the Lewis family, who probably came
from Wales. Owen Lewis, with a name like that, must
surely have been of Welsh ancestry, and was born on 26
March 1844. Migrants frequently integrated with the
indigenous population. Dennis Graham and Margaret
Brown were born in Liverpool, in 1801 and 1811
respectively. In about 1839, they had a daughter, also
named Margaret. She barely knew her father, for Dennis
died in 1846 when she was six or seven. When she grew
up, Margaret married Owen Lewis. We will pick up their
story in the next chapter.

The influx of people placed a huge strain on Liverpool.
In the month of March 1847 alone, 50,000 people arrived,
mostly from Ireland. Many were starving. Countless
numbers died on the streets of the overcrowded city, and
in the bulging hospitals and workhouses. Some 300,000
arrived in less than three years at the peak. They slept
twenty to a room in insanitary and foul-smelling lodging
houses and cellars. Services were overwhelmed. Life

expectancy in Liverpool fell at one point to just eighteen years. But within a few years, the new arrivals had been absorbed and the Liverpool health crisis had been brought under control.

We are now moving to another part of Ireland, from where a different branch of the family originates. John Connolly was born in the tiny hamlet of Cornwall, eight miles – or two hours' walk – outside of Wexford in southeast Ireland, some time before 1820. He married a local woman called Margaret Cullin in June 1836. They had a son, Patrick Connolly, who was born in 1840. Connolly was a name with deep roots, with branches all over Ireland, traceable back to at least the sixteenth century. Patrick married a woman called Sarah Dunbar. The Dunbar name seems to have been Scottish in origin, but its Gaelic roots meant that there were strong Irish connections back to times before record keeping began.

Wexford was probably one of the first parts of Ireland to be inhabited, with traces of human settlement going back to 5000 BC. Gaelic tribes were dominant in the fifth century; Christianity arrived at about the same time; then the Vikings from the year 819; and then the Normans invaded and colonised the country from 1169. The Normans built castles and forts, ushering in a period of settlement and relative stability.

But in the seventeenth century there was more turbulence. Once he had finished with Charles I in England in January 1649, an event we touched on earlier, Oliver Cromwell brought his Parliamentary army to deal with rebels in Wexford. He sacked the town on 11 October that year, killing hundreds of civilians, most of them Catholic. Penal laws continued to discriminate against Catholics in Wexford throughout the seventeenth and eighteenth centuries. In late 1709 there was a new influx of Protestant families to the town, from the Palatinate – just down the road from Baden-Württemberg, from where Balthasar Mock had come to Barnstaple.

The original Norman Catholic families who went to Wexford in the 12th century included the Le Roches, later the Roches. William Roche, probably a descendant of the Normans, was born in Wexford some time in the first part of the nineteenth century. He married a woman called Mary Anne Murphy, and they had a son, James Roche, who was born in 1850. James married Christina Neil – also born in 1850, and whose family name also traced a heritage in Ireland amounting to the best part of a thousand years. James and Christina had a daughter, Annie Roche, who we will come back to in the next chapter.

And now we are moving again, back across to England. John Wilkinson was born in Blyth, in Northumberland, in 1827. These are the northern extremities, beyond Newcastle and Sunderland, and just about as far up in England as you can go without becoming Scotland. Blyth does not enjoy a hospitable climate. It is windy all year. There are more wet days than dry ones. And the wettest month is August. It is cold. Hardly ever above 10 degrees at night, even in the summer. There is now an attractive-looking beach, but it can be no accident that many pictures of it focus on the colourful beach huts, the implication being that if you are going to be at the beach, you are really going to want to be in a hut. (Your grandfather Bill's aunt, Mary, and her husband Bobby had one of the huts at one time, an asset they clearly thought necessary for anyone entertaining thoughts of time at the beach.)

So Blyth had its challenges, and it is perhaps not surprising that for most of the last thousand years few people chose the area as the place to scratch a living. The population was sparse. There are rumoured Roman remains in Blyth, and the port operated from about the twelfth century. There was also a local salt industry in the medieval period, with gathering rights granted to the Priory of Tynemouth in 1315. And the Blyth area, in particular the beach at Seaton Sluice just south of the town, was a popular location for witch burning before the eighteenth century. The 1735 Witchcraft Act brought an end to that, finally making it illegal to accuse anyone of possessing magical powers, which is how many of the innocents fingered as witches in previous centuries were trapped and dealt with. As across most of the rest of the country, agriculture and fisheries had for centuries provided the main livelihoods for the few who inhabited the Blyth area. The land was owned by the aristocrats – up to James Radclyffe, the third Earl of Derwentwater, who was executed for treason in 1715 and whose family accordingly forfeited his property. It was bought by businessmen who wanted to develop the coal industry. The dark fuel had been gathered mostly in small quantities for domestic heating for centuries.

Eventually, from the eighteenth century, Blyth began, slowly at first, to take off. Huge quantities of coal were buried all around the area, and the port and sea access to London made it easy to meet the growing capital's insatiable demand. Deeper coal mines were sunk at Cowpen Colliery and Cowpen Square between 1794 and 1804. That instantly brought an influx of working men and their families eager for consistent and better paid – even if dangerous – employment. An Act of Parliament was obtained and Cowpen Quay was erected, and from around 1810 primitive railroads – horse-drawn wagons running along metal rails – were constructed to shift the coal from

the mines to the barges which would take it to London. So
this was the context into which John Wilkinson was born,
and we will pick up his story in the next chapter.

———·———

From the late eighteenth and early nineteenth century, a
minority of working people began to write diaries and other
descriptions of their lives. Hundreds of these accounts,
often recalling their childhood years and how they started
work as ten-year-olds, have survived. (We have yet to find
any written by your ancestors.) They tell a story of brutality,
suffering, poverty and misery: boys experiencing their first
day in a coal mine with no food, shoes or light; memories
of roasting rats for food because there was nothing else;
tragic stories of children's desperately optimistic attempts
to make a meal for their siblings from frozen turnips.
Children's nimble fingers and strong backs were assets in
the factories and mines. There is some suggestion that the
number of children going to school actually fell in the first
decades of the nineteenth century as more went to the
factory instead.

Life in the newly industrialising towns and cities was
harsh. Across the country as a whole, average life expectancy
in 1841 was forty, but in many industrial towns it fell to
as low as twenty-eight. Working days were long, with
autobiographical coal miners in the north-east recalling
how as young children they rose at 4am, walked two miles
to work and then endured an eleven-hour shift down the
pit. The towns were teeming with cess pools, disgusting
communal latrines, dung heaps (from the horses, who still
powered the transport system) as well as with people, fleas,
lice and rats. No wonder there were big cholera outbreaks

in the 1830s and 1850s. These growing urban settlements were freezing in winter, dark at night, smelly and smoky, with coal dust hanging in the air and clogging people's clothes, houses and lungs. And they were violent – partly a by-product of the huge numbers of gin shops and brothels which did a roaring trade. Deprivation, disenchantment and alienation were widespread. The factories were noisy and hot: ear-splitting and suffocating.

A growing labour force kept wages down, with competition for jobs. And many of the new workers were children. But while wages across the economy overall were stagnant or falling, they were better in the textile and mining towns than in agriculture, and that is what brought ever larger numbers of people in, one wave after another.

Wages were also substantially higher, as well as work more regular, in the factories and coal mines than in the old cottage industries. Similarly, labouring on the roads, railways and canals was better paid and work was more consistently available than was the case with (often seasonal) agricultural work. These new jobs meant not just more money but also some escape from the tyrannies many people, especially the young, had suffered as a result of the old master–servant relationship in the agricultural economy. Low levels of employment kept the poorest people at the beck and call of potential employers in the countryside. People found more freedom in the towns and cities.

Few of the accounts written by working people of their early nineteenth-century lives came from women. Girls had fewer educational opportunities than their brothers, and less money for paper, pens and ink. Discrimination and violence, especially of a sexual sort, against women and girls was routine, and the threat or experience of it figures large in the limited number of women's accounts of their lives that were produced. But very gradually things improved for girls too. More found their way into the factories and out of the near slavery that domestic service could amount to. With their own incomes, their control over their own lives and their power to choose husbands for themselves grew.

Something else that becomes clear from working people's own accounts of their lives is their strong interest in love and sex. There is nothing surprising about that. People may have talked about the issues in different, more coded ways, and social norms may have been more conservative than now, but the fundamental urges were just the same. The adolescent diarist Samuel Bamford confessed to being swept off his feet by "heart-gushings of romantic feeling". Robert Anderson admitted he was unable to concentrate at church because of "that girl with the rosy cheeks across the aisle". Elizabeth Oakley told her diary that the new hand on her employer's farm was "the nicest looking young man I had ever seen … he had dark eyes and his hair was black and hanging in shining ringlets around his head". Courtship rituals involved "walking out", a process instigated by boys, gifts of a lock of hair and a pocket handkerchief, and friends acting as chaperones. Privacy for anything more intimate could be hard to find. John Cannon, a farm labourer, wrote that the "odd doings" between him and his employer's maidservant Mary Rose as Mary passed his bed on her way to her own at night were "difficult to be kept long a secret , by reason of the boy", by which he meant the young lad, presumably another employee, with whom he shared the bed.

Sealing the deal and tying the knot had challenges too, including financial ones. The cost of setting up home together was one. Then there was the wedding itself. As another autobiographer, James Nye, put it, "when I agreed to be married I had only one sovereign in my pocket to do everything with … Well, off I went to church with my bride and was married as big as anybody with an empty pocket; at least I came home so, for after I bought a wedding ring and a wedding dinner and paid the parson my money was gone."

By the middle of the nineteenth century a technological transformation had created huge new opportunities. But there was debate and uncertainty at that time over who was benefiting. This is the era captured in the description of factories, into which the masses had poured, as dark satanic mills. John Stuart Mill, a philosopher some of you have read, wrote in 1848 that it was "questionable whether all the mechanical inventions lightened the toil of any human". Certainly, the aristocracy, the manufacturers and the middle classes enriched themselves. But the accounts of working people themselves reveal something else too. Joseph Levy wrote in 1868 that "looking back sixty years I cannot help constantly exclaiming 'What a contrast there is betwixt the present advantages of poor people and their children and that period' (1810)". Similarly, John Bennett, born in 1787, advised his children in the 1850s to "look back and see what troublesome times we had during my bringing up" because "the working classes now was never so well off". The past was routinely described as "the bad old times".

The improvement was partly material: there was more work, it was more regular and incomes as a result were consistently higher. That translated directly and especially into more and better food. Working-class memoirists also painted a picture of a host of other material improvements, like how plates, basins and metal spoons had replaced the clumsy wooden bowl. But progress went beyond material change. Importantly, it started to break forever the servile submission in which poverty had enslaved people like your ancestors to rural bigwigs for centuries. And things were about to take a dramatic turn for the better.

4

Beyond Poverty: The Second Half of the Nineteenth Century

in which, finally, the Mocks leave Devon for London, the Lowcocks establish themselves in St Helens, where we also meet the Thomas family originally of Holywell, the Watsons fuse with the Gillbankses and prosper in Watermillock, the McGuinness, Rudd and Lewis families congregate in Liverpool, we catch up with the Connollys in Wexford, learn more of the Wilkinsons in Northumberland, and the Swedish and Baltic branches of the family come to light.

Most of what we know for sure about your forebears up to the middle of the nineteenth century comes from just one source: the parish records of births, marriages and deaths which were kept for centuries in churches all over the country. They tell us the bare facts of people's names and essential dates. It takes quite an effort to unearth that information, often involving squinting for hours on end at ancient microfiche in records offices around the country. Your grandfather Bill has done his share of that. I did some nearly forty years ago, for other purposes, and it was no more enjoyable then. My cousin Steve Connolly got his accountant to do it, which is how the bones of the Mocks' story back to the 1550s were uncovered.

Your ancestors were not the sort of people who had their portraits painted, wrote diaries or achieved such fame and fortune that they found their way into the history books, so the sources of information are quite limited. Some of them may have written letters, which was the main way people communicated with others out of shouting distance up to the late nineteenth century and beyond. But no such family letters have survived – or at least none have been uncovered so far. We do have quite a lot of general information about people like your ancestors who lived in the mid-nineteenth century and earlier. And what we have done so far in this story is infer from that general knowledge about life for people like your forebears, to make educated guesses about the lives of your ancestors themselves.

From the second half of the nineteenth century, however, we have quite a lot more information. First, the regular ten-yearly census of the whole population of Britain and Ireland, which was conducted from the early nineteenth century onwards, yields increasing amounts of information by the middle of the century. The members of each household, their ages, occupations, addresses, and, by the end of the period, any disabilities or infirmities they had are recorded. The handwriting of some of the enumerators is less legible than for others. But more and more of the records are also searchable online, which might not be your personal top idea of fun but is, I can tell you, way ahead of schlepping around records offices all over the country.

And if we know where people lived, we can consult Mr Google to see what their houses and streets actually look like, provided – as is surprisingly often the case – they still exist.

Second, photography, invented in the first half of the nineteenth century, became by the latter stages of the century sufficiently widespread and affordable that ordinary people like your forebears could have family or individual portraits taken. There are a few remaining black-and-white photos of some of your great-great-great-grandparents. Stiff and starchy they and their clothes may look to us, but a sense of the people and their personalities still comes through.

And third, you know people who themselves knew some of your late nineteenth-century forebears. Your grandparents have memories, mostly from the 1940s, of some of their grandparents. At that stage, the grandparents' grandparents were quite ancient, but they had lived their early lives at the back end of the nineteenth century and they answered their grandchildren's questions and told them stories, some of which have been retained.

Better information was not the only advance of the second half of the nineteenth century. This was, in fact, a half century in which life improved more for ordinary British people than in any other fifty-year period in the whole of human history up to that point (all 150,000 years of it). First of all there was an amazing improvement in physical infrastructure. Roads, sewers, bridges, viaducts, the telegraph system, gas lighting, safer drinking water, schools, hospitals, libraries, town halls, museums, concert halls, railway lines – and stations – as well as churches appeared all over the country. Some 1.5 million new houses were built in the twenty years after 1850 alone.

Science and technology produced quite an array of innovative new products. The sewing machine arrived in 1846. The elevator in 1852, followed seven years later by the escalator. Then came the typewriter in 1867, the telephone in 1876, the wind-up gramophone in 1887, the first camera using roll film in 1888 and the humble paperclip in 1899. In the middle of all this, in 1873, came a little innovation its inventor Christopher Sholes would be staggered to see you, me and hundreds of millions of other people using every day, and much more than in his own time – the QWERTY keyboard.

Governments proposed and Parliament passed countless laws to improve the lot of ordinary people. Laws were introduced to protect workers, reduce working hours, reduce child labour, improve building standards (so all those new homes were not just new but also better), safeguard public health, extend the right to vote (and, equally important, get rid of a lot of the corruption baked into the previous arrangements by facilitating more political competition) and in many other areas of life. The move towards towns accelerated further. That meant more choice over work, new leisure and social opportunities and easier access to the growing variety of goods in the shops. Working people keeping diaries talked about how fast life was improving in many towns and cities.

The number of people relying on poor relief fell. That was brutally accelerated by the 1834 Poor Law, much less generous for many of the most defenceless and vulnerable people than its predecessor, with less emphasis on cash handouts and more on the workhouse. One of the most regrettable consequences of that was that families and couples were split up. Disraeli, one of the leading Tory statesmen of the nineteenth century said the Act "disgraced the country". But the fact remained that many people were getting substantially better off. In 1815, 15 per cent of the population had needed help under the poor laws; by the 1890s it was just 3 per cent. The highest wages for working people were still to be found in coal mining and factories, which proved to be particularly to the advantage of your ancestors in Lancashire and Northumberland.

In rural areas wages lagged. That created incentives for even more migration from the countryside, where people were still oppressed and dirt poor, to the towns, where they might hope to be a bit better off and have a tad more choice over their own lives. There were simply more and better opportunities in towns and cities, and that no doubt was one of the things that set Edward Mock, whose story we will pick up momentarily, on his way. He was one of the 1.6 million rural people who moved to London and industrial towns in the sixty years after 1851. Another 600,000 relocated to coal mining areas, including the Thomas family from Holywell, north Wales, who we will meet shortly. Growing wages were moreover accompanied by falling prices for food, especially as a result of cheap grain and meat imports, with the new invention of refrigeration meaning that livestock products could now be brought from as far afield as Australia. But it was not just about imports. There was more home-grown culinary creativity too. Fish and chips as a meal was invented, apparently in Oldham in the 1860s.

Clothes evolved in the nineteenth century. Women started wearing underwear. Knickers commenced at the waist and extended down to the knee. Legs were not on display: skirts remained long. They frequently bulged outwards as they reached the floor, further or less far as fashion swayed to and fro. Trousers arrived for men, along with one-piece undergarments stretching from ankle to neck and wrist. Everyone wore hats, segregated according to the class divide: top hats for the wealthy, bowlers for the middle classes, and cloth caps for your ancestors and their ilk. Children – of the better off at least – finally had their own sorts of clothes, rather than just smaller versions of what their mothers or fathers wore. Fashion evolved further with technology. Elastic in 1820, safety pins in 1849 and zips in 1893 all created new opportunities to experiment. People bought more and better clothes; not least women, and not least to attract men.

They also invested more in furnishings, furniture and domestic comforts. The consumer product that saw the single biggest growth in expenditure, however, was tobacco. Smoking progressively became ubiquitous, certainly among men, spawning a noxious century of poisoned air and disease only recently and even now incompletely ended. On the other hand, some vices were reduced: the consumption of alcoholic spirits fell by 80 per cent and that of beer by 40 per cent in the 60 years from the 1870s, a notable achievement of widely supported temperance movements.

There were also important social changes. The number of married women working began to fall, which had significant benefits for child-rearing and child health. The status and prospects of children were further enhanced by rapid expansion in education. By the end of the century, essentially every child went to school, normally to the age of at least fourteen. School attendance became a legal requirement by 1880, which helped wrap in the laggards, but most parents had sent their children there already. Literacy, accordingly, became almost universal. Expansion of education benefited girls as well as boys, so gender discrimination began slowly to be eroded.

There was a wide expansion too in leisure activity. People wanted friendships, conviviality and fun, and had more time and money to organise them as incomes rose. Croquet, badminton, football, rugby and tennis were all developed between 1850 and 1870. In 1893 rugby league, which your grandfather later watched growing up, was created for the working class of the north-west as a result of a split from the rugby union hierarchy. Cricket, horse racing and golf spread. At the end of the nineteenth century, Liverpool had 212 football clubs and 242 cricket clubs, to the enjoyment of several of your male forebears. Organised sport was, some people thought, the greatest cultural invention of the Victorians.

Reading, plays and the music hall were other mass occupations. Satire, stories and poetry were all popular. Charles Dickens was one of the most famous (and richest) people in the country, with huge numbers of ordinary people devouring each weekly or monthly instalment of his books or going to his readings. He did a good deal to spread literacy before schooling was compulsory, as people saw the pleasure to be gained from reading and were prompted to learn.

Alongside government action, a wide variety of new social institutions came into being. They were as diverse as the Mothers' Union (founded in 1886), friendly societies (for mutual self-help and saving), and the Lake District Defence Society of 1883 (predating the founding of the National Trust in 1895). Medical insurance schemes expanded to cover more of the population, and, as we will come to, doctors finally learned a few more procedures that actually prevented and cured disease and illness. Early mortality fell, life expectancy grew. Women's health, though, remained full of taboo. Women were encouraged

to sustain a life-threatening modesty, with many of them
– and their doctors – still believing in the middle of the
nineteenth century that menstruation, which was rarely
mentioned explicitly, was a disability, not a normal event.

Values and behaviour changed too. Recorded crime,
violence – including, apparently, domestic violence – and
murder all fell. Petty theft of food and clothing – stealing
from the poor by the poorer – fell from the 1880s. As more
people became better off, they were less often reduced to
desperate measures. Embezzlement and fraud, by contrast,
those crimes of the educated and avaricious, became bigger
problems. Respectability was the watchword, reinforced
by the church, the courts and the mid-century invention
of the regulated national police force. As one historian
put it, working people wanted to create security, safety
and cleanliness. Sunlight soap was one of the first mass-
produced goods. Appearances were to be kept up, social
status was to be asserted, and children were to be raised
according to ideals, with a clear distinction between the
roles of men and women.

All this went alongside a growing assertion of rights,
promulgated in particular by newly forming trades unions,
and reflected in the growing but still far from complete
expansion of the right to vote. That said, jingoism, bigotry
and intolerance remained universal. Political rights for
women were not on the agenda. When Prime Minister
Gladstone in the late 1880s said he could not accept
women voting because they were too pure and refined for
the vulgarities of politics, the general reaction, even among
women themselves, was not that he was an antediluvian
reactionary. People just nodded sagely.

In the middle of the century, three million women and
girls over the age of ten were at work, 750,000 of them

as domestic servants. Domestic service remained a growth industry for decades afterwards, an indicator of growing inequality in income and wealth. Women in factories were paid only half what men received. More women stayed at home after they married. Family size also fell, with the average number of children per long-term marriage falling from six to four in the fifty years from 1860. Edward Mock, by illustration, had five children in the late nineteenth and early twenty centuries, compared with the thirteen his father sired. There was also a dramatic fall in illegitimacy, which had been rising since the beginning of the eighteenth century. Peaking in around 1850, it reached its lowest ever level in 1901 before rising again.

There also seems to have been an important evolution in what people knew and believed about sex, and in sexual practice. It was, for example, commonly believed at this time that women could only get pregnant if they had an orgasm. The development of rubber vulcanisation technology led to the production of better condoms, which became increasingly popular, at least in the cities, from the 1870s. They were given impregnable respectability by the fact that the packaging featured full-colour portraits of Gladstone and Queen Victoria, who is known to have enjoyed her sex life. Victorian attitudes were not really a Victorian phenomenon, as we will reveal later on: they peaked more than fifty years after she died.

Holidays spread to factory workers, who like miners were better paid than many other workers. Blackpool boomed, aided by the introduction of bank holidays to provide a day off from work for everyone from 1871. One of the unexpected and unplanned spin-offs of the creation of the textile towns was that people played together as well as worked together. They congregated in brass bands, sports teams and on day trips on bank holidays. People travelled further from home – a consequence of the railways and higher incomes – and came to see how they were both similar to and different from their countrymen in other regions. A greater awareness began to spread of how accents varied across the country, for example.

Let us now pick up the stories of those of your ancestors we met in the last chapter. The second half of the nineteenth century is when many of the sixth generation lived the last phases of their lives. For the seventh generation, many of whom were born around the middle of the century, this was prime time. And most of the eighth generation grew up and had their early adult lives in the late nineteenth century, straddling over into the new century.

This is the period of history in which we have found the largest numbers of your forebears. We have identified more than sixty people in the sixth, seventh and eighth generations, many of whom we are about to introduce. Why is this the largest group? Clearly, as you go back each generation, you have twice as many ancestors. You have two parents, four grandparents, eight great-grandparents (who we will call G1s), sixteen great-great-grandparents (G2s), thirty-two G3s, sixty-four G4s and so on.

Actually, it is not quite as simple as that, because the further back you go, the more likely it is that some people are in more than one line of the family. That is because, for example, some of the G3s may have one or more of their own grandparents in common. We will see a possible example of that phenomenon when we get back to the Lewis clan in Liverpool. And by the way, the further back you go, the bigger an issue this becomes. If you think about it for a moment, that becomes obvious: if you were to keep going doubling the number of ancestors every generation, you ultimately end up with trillions of theoretical ancestors, which is a much bigger number than there are people who have ever lived. So family trees which keep forking outwards as you go back from the present through the first few generations, start eventually to fork back together again. Statisticians have in fact worked out something even more remarkable: that if you go back far enough in the history of a human population, you reach a point in time when all the individuals who have any descendants among living people are ancestors of all living people.

Nevertheless, it is the case that in the three-hundred-year period we are dealing with, each generation you go back further into the past contains more of your direct ancestors than the one it gave birth to. The further back in time we go, however, the less good the records are. And because of that, the further back we go, the fewer people we can find. Hence, while we have identified all sixteen people who were your G2s, and twenty-six of the (probably) thirty-two people who were your G3s, we have only identified twenty-five of the (up to) sixty-four people who could have been your G4s. Only sixteen of the G5s. And just five of the G6s. By the time we get all the way back to the G10s, we can find only three of them. In total, in this story, we meet 122 of your ancestors, or 124 including me and your mum. And more of them, members of the sixth, seventh and eighth generations (your G2s, G3s and G4s), appear in this chapter on the second half of the nineteenth century than in any other chapter. That makes the next few pages quite busy. In order to make it a bit easier to see who is who, I have listed all their names

Patrick Connolly, seventh generation, Wexford circa 1890.

Sarah Dunbar, seventh generation, Wexford circa 1890.

Newly married Jack Connolly and Annie Roche, eighth generation, Wexford, circa 1900, just before emigrating to London.

Julia Turtle, eighth generation, Liverpool, circa 1940s.

Tom Watson, eighth generation, Watermillock, circa 1910.

Isabella Abbott, eighth generation, Watermillock, circa 1910.

Richard Rudd, eighth generation, with daughter Emily, who was a GI bride, circa 1940s.

Edward Mock, eighth generation, London, circa 1900.

Edward Mock and Alice Humphrey (eighth generation), with daughters Elsie (l) and Rene (r), ninth generation.

Peter Lewis and two younger brothers,
ninth generation, circa 1920.

*(L to r) Mary, Nance and Florence
Wilkinson, ninth generation,
in the garden at 5, Short Row,
Isabella Colliery, 1920s.*

*The car that Tom
(ninth generation) built,
Watermillock, with (l) his father
Tom Watson in the rear seat,
circa 1930.*

Pat Connolly and Elsie Mock, ninth generation,
south-east London, circa 1932.

Peter Lewis and Mary Rudd
(ninth generation), Liverpool, 1937.

Tom and Florrie Watson, near Watermillock,
possibly during honeymoon.

Knotts Sawmill, Watermillock.

and which generation they come from in the Appendix at the end of the book. And with that introduction, here goes.

The last time we were with the Mocks, in 1863, the latest John Mock and his wife Mary had just welcomed their baby son Edward. It was Edward who finally got your Mock ancestors out of Devon, two hundred years after Balthasar had arrived there.

John and Mary had six children. Edward was the youngest. After Mary's death, John remarried; his new wife, Elizabeth, was seventeen years younger than him and together they had seven more children, all born in Georgeham. Edward is identified in the 1881 census as a seventeen-year-old agricultural labourer lodging with the Anderton family in Trimstone near Barnstaple. He was, evidently, not living at home. The story that has been passed down speaks to some sort of family bust-up which ended in Edward moving out. Though obviously not, initially, very far. Trimstone is eleven miles north-west of Barnstaple, and only four miles from Georgeham.

But that was just the beginning. Ten years later, we find Edward again. And now he is married, to Alice, who had been born in Chiswick in 1866, the daughter of Thomas Humphrey and Annie, formerly Ann Ball. (Thomas and Annie had eight children in all.) Thomas, born in about 1825, had at the time of Alice's birth been working as a cashier in a brewery. The Humphreys were from Buckinghamshire, where Thomas' father, also Thomas, and mother, Mary, had both been born in 1796. Edward and Alice got married on 1 September 1890 at St Matthew's Church, Brixton, then part of Surrey. He, at twenty-six, was working as a barman (or a potman as it was sometimes called then, on account of the beer being served in pots) and his wife Alice was a dressmaker, just as her mother had been. They lived in two rooms at 8 Station Terrace in Denmark Hill, in south London. By 1891 the census tells us that Alice and Edward were living in Lambeth, with her mother and Sidney Humphrey, who may have been Alice's brother.

When we left them in 1845, John Lowcock had just married the twenty-two-year-old Sarah Winstanley in Burnley. Within a few years they had moved to St Helens. Their son, John Albert Lowcock, was born there in 1852. He subsequently married Mary Lewis, who had been born in 1856. She eventually died in 1904, though her husband John lived until 1916. Mary Lewis may have been an example of the phenomenon I described earlier, of the forks of the family tree moving together again the further back you go. In other words, this Mary Lewis, who was marrying into the Lowcock family, may possibly have been part of the Lewis family of Liverpool who we have been following, and one of whom, Peter Lewis, born in the early twentieth century, was your great-grandfather. There may have been similar examples among the Wilkinsons of Blyth, who we will also come back to shortly.

John and Mary had a son, James Lowcock, born in St Helens in 1882. He married Ada Anderson. According to the 1901 census James was at that time a coal miner. He had two sisters, Mary and Betsy. We know a little more of the background of Ada Anderson. She was born in 1881, in Liverpool. Her father, Frank (christened Francis) Anderson, had been born in Sweden in 1847. He seems to have arrived in Liverpool as a sailor in the early 1870s. Ada's mother, Elizabeth, had been born in 1851, one of six siblings. In the 1871 census, Elizabeth is registered as living in the Rotherham household in Liverpool, and working as a servant.

By 1881, Frank was working as a labourer and living with Elizabeth and their family at 17 Avison Street in Toxteth, which was registered as a chandler's shop (a place where sailors could buy what they needed for voyages). Elizabeth was in 1881 listed as the keeper of the shop. That could explain how Frank, originally a sailor, and Elizabeth, a shopkeeper selling sailor's items, met. The couple then had three children, Rachel, Mary and Samuel. Ada was to be born later in 1881. More children – young Frank, Louisa and Rebecca – came along later in the 1880s. In 1891 the census records the family as living at 53 York Street in St Helens. The elder Frank (Francis) was then working not as a sailor or a casual labourer, as he used to, but at a chemical factory. Ada – like young Frank and Louisa – was at school. Samuel was a shop assistant.

We do not have much information about the forebears of Mary Thomas, who was to marry into the Lowcock family in 1933. We know she was of Welsh stock. Her father, John Thomas (the oldest member of the family included in a photograph in which I too appear), came with his family from Holywell in Flintshire in the late nineteenth century to work in the mines around St Helens. Mary Thomas' mother was Margaret Davies, also a very Welsh-sounding name. She was also from Holywell.

Holywell, on the west side of the River Dee, is on the path the crow would take flying from Liverpool to Snowdonia. It was occupied from Roman times, and attracted religious and tourist attention on account of St Winefride's Well, whose water was long believed to have a tonic effect. In the eighteenth century, a small community developed, making a living from lead mining, cotton milling and copper production. Holywell was called a market town, but never amounted to a great deal – even at the start of the current century the population was only 6,000. There are still people there with the Thomas family name. But of course there are huge numbers of Welsh people with the same name, and while your grandfather Brian's memory is that both his mother's and father's forebears were from Holywell as far back as people knew, we have not yet definitively identified any of John Thomas' forebears. It seems a fair bet that they were Welsh centuries back. But beyond that, who knows?

Let us now return to the Watsons in the Lake District. In March 1859, at the age of forty, Joseph married Isabella Gillbanks. (The Gillbanks name was kept going by its adoption as a middle name for sons in later generations right down to your grandfather Bill.) Isabella was the daughter of William Gillbanks, who had married the twenty-nine-year-old Margaret Plasket in Threlkeld in May 1824. Eight or ten years later (there is some uncertainty) Isabella was born. In 1881, at sixty-one years old, Joseph was the innkeeper at the Brackenrigg Inn. He also had a successful carpentry business, and he farmed eleven acres, probably mostly for fruit and vegetables. Joseph and Isabella had a son, Thomas, and then another, Joseph, whom they gave the middle name Todd, after Joseph senior's paternal grandmother Mary Todd.

The Brackenrigg Inn – which we have described earlier – has been going for hundreds of years and is still open today. Your grandfather Bill remembers in the late 1950s seeing the name of a Joseph Watson on the notice above the door, indicating the identity of a current or possibly previous landlord. That was probably Joseph Todd Watson. In the 1881 census, when Joseph senior was the landlord, his son Joseph Todd, then nineteen, was described as a general inn servant and pot boy. It would have been natural, therefore, for him later to have taken on the inn from his father. Joseph senior died in 1885. He and Isabella, who lived another five years, had left a good legacy – not huge riches, but a foundation, material goods and businesses to pass on and, even more important, skills, capabilities and values which would enable the subsequent generations to flourish.

Joseph Todd Watson's older brother Thomas, who had learned joinery and carpentry, no doubt from his father, inherited that business, as well as turning his hand to painting and decorating. He also inherited the Gillbanks name and passed it on further down the family. At times when the population was growing, and the economy was doing well, there were plenty of opportunities for joiners. The late nineteenth century saw the beginnings of a fifty-year period in which the standard of living for many working- and middle-class people across the country was transformed: transport systems, housing, plumbing, the arrival in many homes of electric power and light, and with them the gradual spread of powered consumer durables, the telegraph and radio, and the better food, clothing and entertainment that all these things made possible. This was an era when many people could afford to improve their houses, or have new ones built. Thomas, as a joiner, was therefore in a good line of work.

Born around 1860, Thomas married Isabella Thompson Abbott. Isabella was from a Lake District family too. Her father Christopher was born in Mungrisdale, a few miles north of Ullswater, and her mother Jane Wilson in Penruddock, just two miles from Mungrisdale. Tom and Isabella had two daughters who died early in childhood. Amy, another daughter, was born in Watermillock in 1889. Nannie Gertrude, a fourth daughter, was born in 1890.

Then came yet another girl, Clara. So, by the turn of the century, Tom and Isabella had had five daughters. They were all no doubt much loved and enjoyed by their parents. But there was no son. Would the family name continue down the line? Just as now, many did not.

James and Susan McGuinness, originally both from the tiny settlement of Cavanagh in County Cavan, were by 1858 living in Birkenhead, across the Mersey river from Liverpool city centre. They had a daughter, Susannah, born in Birkenhead in 1858. When she was eighteen, in May 1876, Susannah married Richard Rudd, who was two years older, at the church of Our Lady of Reconciliation de la Salette. Richard was from a Liverpool family: his mother, Jane, had been born in Wigan in about 1824.

Richard and Susannah Rudd had a son, also Richard, in November 1883. That Richard was subsequently to marry Sarah Riley. Her father, Martin, had been born in Dublin in 1843, but by 1891 he had joined the exodus from Ireland, and was married to another Jane and working in Liverpool as a labourer. The story that Sarah Riley's daughter, Mary Rudd, later told her children (who included your grandmother Marie) was that Martin had come from Ireland with a horse and cart loaded with the contents of a shop, setting up for business initially near the docks where they disembarked in Liverpool and then in more formal premises further into the city. Martin and Jane's eldest son, William, was a tobacco factory hand. Their daughter Sarah, born in about 1887, was the fifth child and fourth daughter.

On a dank Liverpool autumn day – it was 22 October 1859 to be precise – at the ancient church of Our Lady and St Nicholas, Owen Lewis married Margaret Graham. Our Lady and St Nicholas was the Anglican parish church right in the heart of the city, and had been a place of worship for at least 600 years. It was subsequently destroyed by bombing during the Second World War, but was rebuilt thereafter and still remains a cherished Liverpool landmark. We introduced Owen and Margaret briefly in the last chapter. They were the current generation of the Lewis family who were Liverpudlians throughout the nineteenth century. They had a son, John Edward Lewis, born on 29 December 1864 (and going on to survive until 1933). Like many from the city, John Edward made a living as a sailor early in his working life. He married Mary Ann Busch (1865–1934) two days after Valentine's Day in 1888. They lived for a while at 23 Ellison Street, between the Old Swan and West Derby districts, just adjacent to the city centre. (The street, including Victorian and Edwardian terraced houses, is still there, and you can find pictures of it on the internet.)

Mary Ann's father, Augustus Busch, had been born in about 1836 in Prussia, a vast country covering what today is Germany, much of Poland and the Baltic states. Like his later son-in law, he was a mariner, and probably came to Liverpool from one of the Baltic ports. It is unsurprising that in one of the world's great port cities of the time, many of your forebears – including Frank Anderson, John Edward Lewis and Augustus – made a living off the sea. And several found their way to Liverpool from foreign parts as mariners. It's not clear exactly what brought Augustus in. But the 1850s were tumultuous years in Prussia, with financial crashes interspersed with political chaos. Liverpool, despite all its problems, to which we will come, must have been an attractive option. Augustus met and in 1864 married Mary Ann Crawford, whose family had been in Liverpool since at least 1808. The younger Mary Ann, named, obviously, after her mother, was born the following year. By 1881 Augustus was widowed and the younger Mary Ann may have delayed her own marriage to help look after her father and other family members.

Peter Turtle and Elizabeth Farrell were born in Ireland. Peter, who was one of your great-great-great-grandfathers, was born in 1855 and was named after his father. They were from Drogheda, Louth, 30 miles north of Dublin and near what was to become the border area between Northern Ireland and Ireland. Elizabeth, also born in 1855, was from Granard, Longford, west of Dublin. Peter and Elizabeth were both born after the worst of the famine years of the 1840s and early 1850s, during which their parents obviously stayed in Ireland and survived. But the famine hung heavy in the memory, and everyone would have known and heard stories of people who had made better lives emigrating to other countries. And hence the exodus from Ireland continued. Many poorer people who survived the famine were pushed off their rural tenancies as the landowners sought to improve the economics of their enterprises by increasing the size of farms. In Peter and Elizabeth's case, their Irish home areas had been badly affected by the famine. It is therefore not surprising that like many others they took the escape route to Liverpool.

The docks were the heart of Liverpool in the second half of the nineteenth century. They were where all immigrants arrived and many subsequently worked. Contemporaries thought them one of the world's great spectacles. The wharves were piled high with wheat, bacon, cotton, tobacco, sugar, rum, timber of all descriptions from oak and mahogany to walnut, Welsh slate, paving stones and manufactured goods from pitchforks to clothes pegs, from prams to pianos. All of it coming from and going to, as one late nineteenth-century observer put it, "every port in the civilised world, from Yokohama to New Orleans, Honk [*sic*] Kong to San Francisco". Liverpool then was a maritime giant, and almost half of Britain's imports – and one sixth of the whole of the world's cargo – were being handled there. It was the "port of a thousand ships". The docks covered 1,600 acres and thirty-five miles of riverfront. The lucky few made themselves stupendously rich on the back of it all. Your ancestors were not among them.

Some of them were, though, among the thousands of dockers who tried to make a living there every day at the back end of the nineteenth century. It was not a very good living, even by the low standards of the time. The port was still in the early twentieth century considered "the last refuge of the unfortunate". Better, if more dangerous, to be a coal miner. Or better still a (preferably skilled) factory worker. Surplus labour kept wages low, and dockers were hired by the day, and often just for a few days a month. Hundreds milled round every morning hoping to be taken on. Frustration could overflow when they were not. Strikes and riots were common, not least after trades unions enabled workers to organise themselves better to argue their case with the employers. But dockers were as proud and thoughtful as anyone else, and there was a lot of banter and dark humour, with laughter a form of self-defence and sometimes the only affordable pleasure.

Living conditions were nasty. Families shared a room or two in stinking slums, furnished with a few sticks. Here is a newspaper description from the 1890s: "a round deal table with three legs, two or three chairs of various build and design, a couple of stools, a dresser for the few plates and dishes required, and a few soiled prints on the wall, these in the kitchen, with one shaky four poster and a few wretched mattresses in the room above"; these "constitute all in the world that the poor man [a docker] possesses in the shape of household goods. Here he and his wife live and his children are born and reared week in, week out, for year end to year end, where the sun never shines, nor the fresh breezes blow, nor the wild bird sings nor the flower smiles but where instead malarious gases and foul atmospheres permeate every room".

But, the reporter went on, "the home of the labourer, poor and unwelcome as it generally is, is not always a wretched one. Even in these dismal courts may be occasionally found a happy little home, brightened by a smart tidy little wife and a sober, studious husband who after his day at the docks takes home his *Echo* [the local paper] or his *Express* and reads it at his own fireside, or helps his children learning their morning school lessons".

Life in Liverpool then may certainly look tough to us now. But let's remember, people kept coming to the city, not least from Ireland and Wales, and it kept growing. And they never, among your ancestors, who were quite typical in this, seemed to have gone back, except on very rare occasions to visit those left behind. So for all that life was hard in the city, there was hope it could get better, and it was already preferable to what many people had left behind. As we will see, things evolved further by the middle of the twentieth century.

John Connolly and Annie Roche, both of whose families had been in Wexford in south-east Ireland for hundreds of years, as we saw in the last chapter, were the last generation of their family to grow up there. Wexford was one of the parts of Ireland least affected by the potato famine. Their parents had survived it and stayed. Agriculture had always formed the basis of the Wexford economy, as it still does. The sea port was also successful up to the beginning of the twentieth century, when it was undermined by the constantly changing sands. The cost of dredging gradually made it economically unviable. Through the late nineteenth century, the town survived rather than prospered. So it is not surprising that as the generations passed, and better opportunities opened up elsewhere – and with improved communications were increasingly known about and visible – the enterprising young struck out to make their way elsewhere. John and Annie, both born in the mid-1870s, were a couple just about as Irish as it was possible to be, but when they married they moved to London, joining the great throng of Irish people through the nineteenth century who left in the hope of a better life elsewhere.

John Wilkinson was crushed in a mining accident on 25 July 1871. He died the following day of his injuries, inflicted, the record says, "by a fall of stone", which means he was buried by a collapse in the coal face. He was forty-four. And he was your great-great-great-great-grandfather. His widow, Eleanor, and their children had him buried in the Churchyard of St Mary the Virgin, Horton, two miles outside his hometown of Blyth in Northumberland.

Coal was the basis of everybody's living in Blyth. By 1855, 250,000 tonnes a year were being shipped from the town. By 1900 it was a million tonnes. Mining it was dangerous, nasty and life-shortening. But it absorbed huge numbers of working men across the country – there were up to 1.2 million coal miners at the peak early in the twentieth century. And from mining much else followed. Coal helped the cotton industry take off. Without it there would have been no railways. And the invention of the railways was one of the biggest revolutions of the nineteenth century.

In Cowpen and Blyth, major housebuilding programmes improved accommodation from the 1850s. Ultimately, in the twentieth century, the skills built through the mines and the railways, and the coastal location, provided the basis for a local shipbuilding industry. Many Royal Navy ships for the First and Second World Wars were built in and around Cowpen and Blyth, including the first aircraft carrier, the *Ark Royal*, in 1914. The protected waters also provided a submarine base during both world wars. All that – the mines, the railways and the shipbuilding – declined from the 1960s. Very little is left of it now.

There were many mine shafts in the Cowpen/Blyth area in the last decades of the nineteenth century, all dug into the same basic deposit. Several were owned by the Cowpen Coal Company, including the Isabella at Newsham, a mile or so from the original deep shaft at Cowpen. John Wilkinson was working at the Isabella when he died. He was a deputy, meaning his job was to put in place the timber props to protect the miners hewing at the coal face. This was among the more dangerous jobs. And John must have spent much of his life in the pit. He was one of thirty-six men killed in the Isabella mine between 1858 and 1947. Thousands more worked there. One of them, more than fifty years after John was killed, was to become the husband of his great-granddaughter.

But we are in danger of getting ahead of ourselves. John Wilkinson had been born in 1827. He had married Eleanor Nelson. They had a son they named Adam. He married Sarah Hatherick, who was commonly known by her middle name, Hannah. (She was the daughter of Martin Hatherick and a Sarah Wilkinson.) Adam died young, in 1880, the same year that Hannah had a son, who was named Martin after her father. A couple of years after Adam's death, Hannah married his younger brother, David. The census of 1881 records David, then twenty-one, and Hannah (recorded in the census document by her first name of Sarah) as living at 7 Cowpen Square, one of the new dwellings built to accommodate the mine workers. David worked as a locomotive fireman in the mines – basically shovelling coal into the engine furnace to generate the steam to keep the wheels turning. (No doddle, but probably better than being deep underground.) Hannah was listed as the head of the household, presumably because the house had been Adam's, and she was widowed but had not yet married David. She was making ends meet as a dressmaker.

By 1891, David, now thirty-one, and Hannah, thirty-four, were living at the Isabella, at 4 Old Row (as it was called in the 1891 census, but it was later referred to as Short Row after additional houses were added later in the 1890s). David had progressed to become a colliery engineer. The household amounted to nine people. Martin was by then a young boy, and we will meet him again later.

———

By 1901, the population of the UK had reached 42 million, up from 27 million in 1851, itself a substantial increase from the beginning of the century. But the rate of growth was declining. People were living longer but having fewer children. The birth rate declined by between 25 per cent and 30 per cent between the 1880s and the 1900s. By our standards, poverty was still rife. But the number of people condemned to the deep, life-threatening poverty endemic from the sixteenth century to the middle of the nineteenth century (and in the whole of human history before then) was dramatically lower. Really extreme poverty of that sort by 1900 generally threatened only the ill, the elderly and those who lost their main breadwinner – or the remaining minority still burdened with too many young children. The sections of the population whose lives saw the greatest improvement in the last years of the nineteenth century were the better-off working class – a category including many of your forebears. Incomes for them rose by 30 per cent between 1875 and 1900.

Higher incomes by the end of the century brought vastly more food choices into the zone of affordable possibilities for ordinary people. Oranges, nuts, ham sandwiches, baked potatoes, rhubarb, cherries, fried fish, gooseberries, ice cream, crumpets, ginger beer, pea soup, beef pies, lemonade and mince pies would all have passed the lips of your eighth-generation ancestors. Cadbury's chocolate was starting to reach a mass market, and they enjoyed the benefits of that too. Women also learned to cook it all with the help of best-selling cookery books, like *Mrs Beeton's Book of Household Management*, which sold millions of copies from the 1860s.

The nineteenth century saw important improvements in medicine and health care. The stethoscope was invented in 1816, and thermometers of a usable size in the 1860s. The arrival of cholera in London in the 1830s provided a great – and effective – incentive to improve water and sanitation services. Morphine was developed early in the century, and hypodermic syringes to administer it were in use from the 1850s. Anaesthesia finally arrived: ether was first used to extract a tooth in 1842. Queen Victoria was given chloroform in 1853 to have her latest child, Prince Leopold. And when Joseph Lister started to develop anti-septic techniques in the 1860s, the era finally arrived in which surgeons started to do more good than harm. By 1900, they no longer worked in blood-caked suit jackets in dingy rooms with sawdust sprinkled on the floor to soak up the mess they made. They started wearing face masks, rubber gloves and surgical gowns.

It is, before we move forward again, also worth noting what the eighth generation, born between the 1860s and the 1880s, and in or entering the prime of their lives by 1900, still did not enjoy. The right to vote, for most of them, was still some way off. So was electricity: the first power station delivering electricity to homes began operating in London in 1891. The national grid was not established until 1933. There were accordingly no electric kettles until the 1920s, or washing machines or electric clothes driers until the 1910s. Even once invented, more modern conveniences typically took decades to percolate widely across the population. There were gas stoves, which were quite popular by the 1880s. There was also gas lighting, at least for the middle classes, but most heating was provided by fires, most commonly from coal. The fire was also used to turn water for washing and bathing from freezing to at least tepid, and with luck warmer than that.

A rudimentary water supply to homes began appearing in some parts of cities like Liverpool from the 1840s. But the service was poor and irregular, and carrying water into and around the house remained a huge labour for women and children for decades after that. The modern bathroom did not exist. Water tanks on top of the toilet allowing normal flushing were unavailable, and indeed rolls of toilet paper were not marketed until 1902. London building regulations in the 1890s imposed no requirement for indoor toilets. In fact, plenty of people right up to the 1970s had only outdoor toilets. A surprising number of people then still thought outdoor loos were a lot more hygienic than bringing everything indoors. Some of your grandparents and their siblings – unfortunately including those in the most inclement parts of the country – grew up just with outdoor toilets. They were typically positioned a cold, dark and wet walk down a concrete path from the back door of the house. There was no radio: the human voice was not transmitted wirelessly until 1900. Nor had the cinema been invented. Likewise television. Entertainment was live, and music and concert halls were big businesses where people did a lot of their laughing. And those nocturnal journeys to the loo no doubt also provided a good deal of hilarity, at least for those not embarking on them.

5

The Beginning of Modernity: The Early Twentieth Century

---

in which, between 1905 and 1915, your great-grandparents are born in Liverpool, St Helens, Cumberland, Blyth and London.

Let's summarise where we have got to. On your father's side: the ninth generation, your great-grandparents, came from the Lowcock family, now in St Helens; the Thomas family, originally from north Wales and also now in St Helens; the Mock family, previously of Devon and now of London; and the Connolly family, originally of Wexford and shortly also of London. On your mother's side, they were from the Watson family of Watermillock, the Wilkinsons of Blyth, the Lewis family of Liverpool, and the Rudds, also of Liverpool. At the beginning of our story, almost everyone was a rural dweller; now all bar the Watsons lived in towns and cities. They were all tradesmen and working class. Many, though not all, of the eighth generation, your great-great-grandparents, now found themselves among the better-off working classes, including the coal miners and the factory workers. But they would mostly have been paid weekly, in cash, and lived from one week to the next. Most of your great-great-grandparents had been to school, and many regularly went to church. A few may have had the right to vote (though in 1900 that was still restricted to just 40 per cent of the adult male population). Most drank, many smoked. We know what some of them looked like, from remaining black-and-white photos, where they stand formally in their best clothes and stern faces. One of the problems of early photography was that people had to sit or stand very still, wearing their rictus smiles for several moments, in order to get a reasonably clear take. That, together with the inbuilt formality of the age, added to the staged look of early photographic portraits.

What was the country like, into which the ninth generation were born? We touched on this at the end of the last chapter. For one thing, your great-grandparents may have been the first generation of the family in which everyone was literate, because by the time they were born England had an educational system better than that available to their parents, ensuring that all children had a reasonable degree of formal schooling. It was a society gradually becoming less violent, a development caused less by an outbreak of modern liberal values than by commercial interests. Seaside landladies, publicans, music hall proprietors and football clubs did not want their revenues interrupted by damage or disturbance from too many rowdy customers, and they were able to enforce better behaviour. That said, this Britain was an armed country: anyone could walk into a shop and buy a revolver with no questions asked. And the 1903 Pistols Act, which banned pistol sales to people who were under eighteen or who were "drunken or insane", did little to change that.

Suburbia became a thing in the first part of the twentieth century. The transport system finally meant that people could get to jobs more than walking distance away. The London suburbs absorbed 700,000 new people from 1900 to 1911, many of them, like the Mocks and the Connollys, in the south-east of the city. With suburbia came gardens, and so one of the great hobbies of British people emerged as a mass passion, infecting every generation of your family from your great-grandparents down. Reading and singing were also hugely popular pastimes. This was the period in which classics like *Peter Pan*, *The Railway Children*, *Winnie the Pooh* and a host of other stories of your childhood and mine were written.

There was, though, much that remained of the Victorian era in the country into which the eighth generation had been born. There was huge wealth inequality, with the magnates and the aristocracy enjoying much more power and money than today's hedge fund billionaires. But there were signs that this could not last forever: the National Trust, which over time was to take over many of the grandees' great houses and estates, was given statutory powers in 1907. Class distinctions and hierarchies dominated much of life, even governing what people could wear wandering down the street. A woman wanting to be regarded as respectable dared not venture out of doors without her hat and gloves. A shop assistant could not stroll along the seafront on a Sunday without a jacket for fear of the wrath of his employer the following day. The streets were still overcrowded, smelly and noisy. Horses pulled the omnibuses and cabs, depositing their by-products liberally across every street and pavement and causing as much environmental hazard as the smog from the ubiquitous burning coal. Cycling was now popular but there were next to no cars. Sex outside marriage and illegitimate children were things to be ashamed of, though that did not stop the upper classes or the poorest, whose behaviour caused a good deal of tutting among the middle and better-off working classes.

Let us now introduce the ninth generation, your great-grandparents.

James Lowcock, the coal miner born in St Helens in 1882, and Ada Anderson, the daughter of a sailor and a shopkeeper, seem to have got together early in the twentieth century. By 1911, according to the census that year, Ada was married and living at 53 York Street. That had been her family home as a child, and she was there now with two young children of her own: James Maxwell, known as Jim, aged two, and baby Ada, just four months old. Jim was your great-grandfather. (The elder Ada was described in the 1911 census entry as the head of the household. It is not clear why she was back living in her childhood home, or where her husband James was when the census was taken, but he was not listed at York Street. We will however pick up his story a few years later.)

John Thomas, born in Holywell in 1884, moved to St Helens to work in the mines. Coal had been mined there for hundreds of years. John's family lived in the Thatto Heath area of St Helens, and the story goes that their house was built almost on an opencast mine. So, as your grandfather Brian says, "the family used to dig coal from their garden for their home fires until the local mine owners objected and then they dug it from under the floorboards of the house". St Helens was one of the places where miners first got themselves organised to negotiate better terms and conditions with the mine owners. It was prominent in the establishment of the Lancashire Miners' Federation in 1881, and that contributed to the creation of the Miners' Federation of Great Britain in 1888. In the coal strike of 1912, 850,000 miners stopped working, only going back after most of what they wanted was conceded in Parliament. John married Margaret Davies, who was also from Holywell, and together they had eleven children: Edna, Jim, Annie, Sam, Ethel, Eliza, Vera, Tom, Harry, John and, in 1909, Mary – who was always known as Polly. The reasons for the nickname are now murky, but it may have had something to do with the nursery rhyme, Polly Put the Kettle On. Polly was your great-grandmother.

In 1901 Edward and Alice Mock were living at 31 Napier Street, in Deptford, in south-east London. Deptford is on the Thames, adjacent to the naval college and the Royal Observatory at Greenwich and just across the river from what is today the Canary Wharf financial centre. Edward and Alice's first child, also Edward, had been born in 1895, but died when he was about ten. By 1911, Edward and Alice were living at 121 Reidhaven Road, Plumstead. They had moved east along the river, presumably to afford better and larger accommodation for themselves and their now four children. The house, an attractive yellow-brick two-up, two-down Victorian cottage, is still there. At that time, Edward, previously a barman and before that an agricultural labourer, was working in an arms factory – the Woolwich Arsenal – where they manufactured gun barrels and ordnance. Reidhaven Road was within easy walking distance of the factory. Alice and Edward subsequently moved again, further east once more, to Welling, again for cheaper and newer accommodation. The children were all girls: Florence, born in 1900; Ethel in 1902; Elsie in

1905; and Irene, or Rene as she was always known, who was born in 1908 or 1909. Elsie, then eighty-six, and Rene were at my and your mum's wedding. Elsie was your great-grandmother.

John Connolly (who was known as Jack) and Annie Roche married in 1902, and by 1904 were living in Eglinton Road, Woolwich, in south-east London. He worked at St Nicholas' infirmary in Tewson Road, Plumstead, just down the road from Woolwich. He was a laundry man, and later a uniformed gatekeeper. He was also recorded on the birth certificate of Kitty, one of his daughters, as a public assistance officer, meaning he was involved in the administration of the Poor Law providing relief for those with no means of supporting themselves. St Nicholas' infirmary was originally opened in 1874 as part of the Woolwich Union workhouse. It initially catered for children, pregnant women and the homeless, then later for people with mental health problems. Under the Poor Law at that time local authorities were required to provide accommodation for patients with mental illness. At St Nicholas', like other places, this took the form of padded cells. The facilities at the infirmary were built up over the years. The workhouse was eventually closed and the infirmary became St Nicholas' Hospital. Like much else in the Woolwich area, it was badly damaged by bombing in the Second World War, but it was later rebuilt. It was incorporated into the National Health Service in 1948. In 1951 it was largely absorbed by the British Hospital for Mothers and Babies, which used the premises as an annex for their main facilities. Your grandmother Stella was born at the British Hospital for Mothers and Babies, as indeed, later still, was I. In other words, it turns out that I was born at the hospital where more than fifty years previously my great-grandfather had worked. The hospital eventually closed in the 1980s and the services were absorbed into much better, larger and newer facilities. The original site of St Nicholas' infirmary was largely redeveloped into a modern housing complex, but the NHS retains some of the facilities from where, among other things, children's mental health services are now provided.

During the First World War Jack Connolly worked at the Woolwich Arsenal. One might speculate that he met Edward Mock, who as mentioned earlier was also working there, and that it was as a result of their fathers meeting that Jack's son Patrick, who was born in 1906, met Edward's daughter Elsie. Jack was a member of the Woolwich Catholic Club. He brought his singing voice with him from Wexford, and was well known in south-east London as an accomplished tenor soloist, performing at Lewisham Concert Hall and, rumour (unsubstantiated) has it, the Albert Hall. Jack and Annie had seven children: Kitty, Patrick, Kathy, Jim, Jack, Ben and Bob. Patrick, their first son, who was always known as Pat, was your great-grandfather.

The 1911 census records the then fifty-year-old Tom Watson and his wife Isabella living at Knotts Mill, a field away from the western shore of Ullswater and just off what is now the A592 in Watermillock. Built of local stone and mortar, Knotts Mill was a sizeable property. Your grandfather Bill remembers it from the early 1940s, and it had probably changed little in the intervening thirty years:

"It consisted originally of two living rooms, a scullery and three bedrooms. Integral to it was a combined workshop and stables (with stalls for five heavy horses)...Also on site were two outdoor bucket loos, a coalhouse, cart-lodge/washhouse, with a large copper urn and a fireplace beneath to heat the water, hen house, and chicken coops… The buildings were linked by head-high stone walls, encircling a cobbled yard, with cart wheel gates at the front and a sheet metal field gate at the rear, presumably to allow horses to drag felled tree trunks from the nearby hillsides to the (now defunct) mill."

The "mill" was probably simply a pit over which felled trees were laid, so that they could be cut by two men standing either side of the trunk pulling a long saw to and fro. The timber could then be sold on site or transported elsewhere.

And the inside of the house, which Bill also remembers, had probably changed little as well:

"There was a weak cold water tap in the scullery, stone floors and a combined kitchen/sitting room/dining room with damp distempered walls. A huge dining table, Grandad's desk and his large reclining chair, bookcase, numerous cupboards … and a miscellany of armchairs clustered by the fender in winter… Ascending the stairs to bed, clutching candle, hot water bottle, potty (or bucket), and a jug of water took you past an oil painting of a scary-looking unknown gentleman [*most likely Tom's father Joseph Watson, the mid-nineteenth-century keeper of the Brackenrigg Inn, who we met earlier*].… In each bedroom there was a double bed, marble-topped washstand, fireplace, wardrobe and sash window overlooking the yard."

In case you are wondering what happened to the contents of the bucket loos and potties, they were laid to rest in a small shrubbery at the end of the garden.

Tom was still running a carpentry, joinery and painting business. Bill remembers his workshop in the 1940s:

> "Cobbled floor, horse stalls, workbench and vices, his white carpenter's apron, saw horse, tool chest, snares, a large steel animal trap [*smaller version of a man trap*], hack log [*the base of an oak tree on which logs were split*], a two-handed felling saw, axes, night lines [*multi-hooked fishing lines thrown into the lake*], a sledge hammer."

Tom had a number of employees, and alongside his carpentry and cabinet-making business he also had a successful market garden. We can picture him from Bill's later memory:

> "sitting in his huge, self-made reclining chair, with his pint mug, pince-nez glasses, and gold watch chain … with his top hat and hat box, inkwell and quills, sealing wax and seals and a handheld weighing balance"

all within easy reach. The weighing balance was used to measure out and price the delicate sheets of gold leaf which figured in some of Tom's more ornate pieces.

As well as running the household, Isabella seems to have been a dressmaker. A ledger from 1913–14 records customers and prices, and there was still a treadle sewing machine and a dressmaker's dummy in the house years later. As we noted earlier, Tom and Isabella had five daughters.

Two, Lilian Mary and Florence Annie, died as infants, and their remains are marked by small crosses in the graveyard at Watermillock church (near the rather grander marble gravestone below which their grandparents, Joseph Watson and his wife Isabella – nee Gillbanks – lie).

This was an era in which many people, even from remoter areas like Watermillock, were beginning to move around more. Tom and Isabella's next daughter Amy learned secretarial skills (and, less usefully it transpired, Esperanto, the putative world language which came to nothing) and had office jobs in Manchester. But she returned home to run the household for her father when Isabella died. Nannie Gertrude, a second daughter, who had been born in 1890, was mentally and physically disabled from birth. Her disability was recorded in the 1911 census, which included information about infirmities among the population, something that earlier census exercises had not done. She always lived at home and was looked after by the family. Clara, the final sister, also worked in Manchester for much of her life before coming back to Watermillock. She was a chronic asthmatic. Ultimately, she and Amy lived out their lives in Ulverston. Five daughters: none were to marry. And so no hope of grandchildren. Until, in 1904, along came Thomas William Gillbanks Watson, Tom and Isabella's last child. He was your great-grandfather.

In 1901 David and Hannah Wilkinson were still at 4 Short Row – which was the extended terrace previously called Old Row – at the Isabella Pit in Newsham. The houses sat at the end of the cinder road from Blyth. They were effectively part of the pit complex, overshadowed by the winding gear and slag heaps, which often emitted acrid fumes as the coal waste inside them spontaneously ignited. Short Row was a terrace of ten houses. Each had a kitchen/dining room and a sitting room downstairs and two bedrooms above. The outside walls were dulled by grime from the pit. There were manhole covers by each front doorstep, which were opened to shovel free coal from the mine into the cellars beneath. Across the road were the wash houses and outdoor toilets, adorned with cut-up newspaper pages in lieu of toilet rolls.

By the turn of the century David and Hannah's son Martin had joined what in practice was the family business, working, like his father, as a locomotive fireman at the mine. He was responsible for the tank engine. (Forty years later tank engines were given lasting global fame through the Thomas the Tank Engine stories written by the Reverend W Awdry, with which you are familiar.) Martin is remembered for a thick Geordie accent ("I'm gannin on a tooa tamora," he told his grandson years later when visiting him in Ulverston, meaning he was looking forward to the next day's coach trip round the Lake District), a fondness for snuff and his habit of pouring his tea from cup to saucer to cool it – a preference for cold tea possibly being acquired from years at the pit, where he would take a can from home in the morning which would be cold by the time he got to drink it. He spent his whole life working at the Isabella and was still there in the 1940s. The Isabella's own 100-year life was nearing an end by then: it finally closed in 1966. Martin married Mary Pearson, whose family were also from the area. They had two sons and three daughters, including in 1909 Florence May Wilkinson. She was your great-grandmother.

John Edward and Mary Ann Lewis lived their whole lives in Liverpool. By 1911, they were at 12 Heriot Street, West Derby. The street still exists, but the houses have been replaced over the last century. (The original dwellings may have been destroyed by bombing in the Second World War.) John Edward had given up the sailor's life and was now a dock worker. Three-year-old Agnes Busch, presumably a relative of Mary Ann's father or the child of one of her brothers, was living with them, as well as their own children. Those children included Charles William Lewis, born in 1893 and still alive nearly 80 years later (he died in 1972). The 1911 census reports that Charles, then seventeen, was married to Julia Turtle, and they had a baby son, also named Charles. Julia had been born on April Fool's Day 1892. She and Charles married on 24 October 1910 at St Sylvester's, a Gothic Revival Catholic church, built in 1888 but now no longer in use, in the Vauxhall district of Liverpool. So three generations of Lewises were all together in Heriot Street. Their home was a four-room house and it must have been a squash with the whole family – and sundry others like little Agnes – all sharing the space. It became even more crowded on 18 August 1912, when Charles and Julia had another son, Peter. He was your great-grandfather.

By 1911 Richard and Sarah Rudd were living at 105 Ashfield Cottages, a two-room flat in a tenement block in the city of Liverpool. Richard was working as a "carter" – a general labourer – at the docks, a short walk from Ashfield Cottages. Before the First World War, he found regular work and the family were able to rub along. Sarah was "working", the census says, at home. Four years later, in 1915, Richard and Sarah had a daughter, Mary Rudd. She was your great-grandmother.

So we have now met all your great-grandparents, the ninth generation. In St Helens, just outside Liverpool, Jim Lowcock, born in 1909, was to marry Polly Thomas, also born in 1909. In south-east London, Patrick Connolly, born in 1906, was to marry Elsie Mock, born in 1905. Tom

Watson, born in Cumberland in 1904, would find work in Blyth and marry local girl Florence Wilkinson, who had been born in 1909. And in Liverpool, Peter Lewis, born in 1912, would marry Mary Rudd, born in 1915.

———·———

The seminal event of the early adult lives of the ninth generation was the First World War. It was unquestionably the worst experience the British nation had suffered in 300 years. The first thing to say is that your great-grandparents were all fortunate in their timing. The war killed nine million European soldiers, including one in three of all British men born between 1894 and 1896. Your great-grandparents were too young to be called up. Some of their fathers, however, were not so lucky. Some 60 per cent of men of military age fought, mostly in the trenches in France. By 1918 conscription extended to all men up to the age of fifty. Richard Rudd was away at the front for several years. He never talked about his experience but seems to have been able to put it behind him when he returned. Charles Lewis found himself going to war against his grandfather's homeland. (His mother's father, Augustus Busch, was from Prussia.) Quite how Mary Ann – who lived right up to 1934 – felt about her son going to fight against her father's country one can only imagine. Charles served three years in the Royal Garrison Artillery. That was one of the earlier artillery regiments, which fought at the Somme and in other big battles but mostly sat behind the frontline infantry and fired shells towards enemy territory. Charles returned from the front quite a different personality, his family thought, as certainly did many other young men permanently scarred by the experience.

James Lowcock served between 1914 and 1917 in the 5th Battalion of the South Lancashire Regiment. The battalion was first formed in St Helens in the 1860s. Members of the Pilkington family, who owned the coal mines the Thomas men worked in and founded a big glassmaking business in St Helens, which your grandfather Brian later worked for, were prominent in the ranks of officers in the Regiment. The 5th Battalion was a Territorial Army unit of part-time volunteers before the war, and they had just begun their annual training exercise when the war broke out on 4 August 1914. That winter they were sent to France. They were bombarded with chlorine gas at the battle of Ypres in 1915. They fought at the Somme, and again at the third battle of Ypres in 1917. They took hundreds of casualties: many dead, and even more wounded. Again, we can only speculate as to the effect all this had on James Lowcock.

One household in three across the country suffered a war casualty; one in nine a death. The war was initially quite popular – within its first year, two and a half million British men volunteered and headed off to the trenches. It was genuinely thought to be the war to end all wars. Its popularity was reinforced by notorious atrocities committed by the enemy, notably the German sinking of a huge transatlantic passenger liner, the *Lusitania*, in 1915, in which 1,200 civilians, many of them children, were drowned. Throughout, the fighting men believed they were doing their duty and protecting their families at home: as one soldier wrote to his girlfriend in February 1918, "It's just the thought of you all over there – you who love me and trust me to do my share of the job that is necessary for your safety and freedom … That keeps me going & enables me to 'stick it'."

The war also dominated the lives of those, such as the women and children, who did not fight. As one civilian diary keeper wrote in 1918, "Is there any man, woman or child who does not think of the men in the trenches? Most people are so impregnated by the war that they live with it, they sleep with it and they eat it." And the effects were long lasting; a generation of the wounded and mentally scarred were prominent through the 1920s and 1930s. The loss of a generation of young men also reduced the marriage rates of women. That is perhaps why none of your great-grandfather Tom Watson's sisters married. Such women may, as one writer has put it, have enjoyed lives of friendship and fruit cake, and the company and vicarious pleasures of their wider families, but they missed out on a great deal too.

For the first time, the state was mobilised effectively to look after civilians at home during the war. With the men in the trenches, huge numbers of women came into the workforce, especially into factories, offices and the transport system. They started to wear more practical clothes: shorter skirts instead of great billowing tents, and in some cases even trousers. And moral attitudes evolved further too. When it became clear that the flood of men to the front had left lots of unmarried girls pregnant, their children were declared patriotic war babies and the mothers got help. And perhaps it is no coincidence that this was the decade in which contraceptives stopped being hard to buy outside London and other big cities and started to be sold by every village chemist. The publication by Marie Stopes in 1918 of her book *Married Love* dramatically increased the number of people who had access to basic factual information.

Despite the economic imperative to finance the war, the worst food shortages were avoided, bread was never rationed and the most vulnerable were protected. Indeed, the diets and health of poor women and children got better (as also, by the way, happened during the Second World War). Women got more jobs, and there was no unemployment. Initiatives like the Maternity and Child Welfare Act of 1918 encouraged local authorities to support expectant and nursing mothers. In 1915 rent control, which some people think was the most significant piece of social and economic legislation in the first half of the twentieth century, was introduced. The intention was to protect the spending power of working families. But the longer-term effect was to reduce the supply of rented accommodation and support a huge expansion in private construction, further enabled by the development of the mortgage industry. That eventually meant that many people could for the first time buy their own well-built modern houses.

The war also contributed to the moment – finally – at which all the adults in the family acquired the basic citizenship right to vote for the people who ran the country. Up to 1918, that right was enjoyed only by a small minority of your forebears. But the Representation of the People Act of 1918 finally gave the vote to all men over twenty-one. And, in the real departure, to all women over thirty, of whom there were 8.4 million. It took more than ten years for the voting age for men and women to be equalised. (It was not until 1969 that the voting age was reduced, for both men and women, to eighteen.) Another 1918 Act, the Sex Disqualification Removal Act – just look at that name – also opened jury service, the magistracy and the legal profession to women. These developments owed a lot to the pressure and sacrifices of suffragettes before the war, but the war itself probably accelerated matters. All that said, there remained plenty of blatant abuses in the political system. David Lloyd George, one of the most famous prime ministers of the twentieth century, notoriously sold honours for his own personal financial gain. You could get a knighthood for £330,000 (in today's money). These days they give them away for free.

6

Material Progress
and Freedoms:
The Interwar Years

---

in which your great-grandparents get educated,
join the workforce, marry and start their families.

The interwar years are often remembered for the
General Strike in 1926, the Wall Street Crash of
1929 and the mass unemployment of the 1930s.
In fact, the story is more complicated than that. This time
was one of substantial material improvement in the lives of
your great-grandparents. Our ninth generation, like other
working people across the country, enjoyed the benefits of a
huge consumer boom, dramatic improvements in housing,
more access to electricity and water, and an entertainment
revolution.

It was, though, also an era of social and economic
volatility. A pandemic, the Spanish Flu, killed between
a quarter and half a million people – around 1 per cent
of the total population – in 1918–19. Most of the losses
were among younger people, especially pregnant women.
A brief post-war economic boom was rapidly followed

by a crash. Unemployment doubled to two million in just six months from late 1920. It remained a persistent problem throughout the decade – and then it got worse. It was exacerbated in the 1920s by a foolish obsession with maintaining the value of the sterling exchange rate against the dollar. That made imports cheap and exports expensive, so threatening the viability of many domestic industries.

Politicians talked about the need to build homes fit for the families of those eighth-generation heroes who had fought the war. But it was a slow business. An estimated half a million working-class houses were needed in England and Wales in 1919. Many were built, especially on new estates on the edges of towns and cities, though it took years. And standards were mixed. Gas lighting and electricity were generally included. But insulation was poor so that water tanks often froze in winter making toilets unusable. The arrival of electricity began a major transformation in the quality of domestic life, especially for women, who still did all the housework. Over the following decades, kettles, vacuum cleaners, toasters, electric stoves, irons, sewing machines and later fridges and washing machines would become more and more common in the homes of working-class families like those of your great-grandparents. But all the modern conveniences – mod cons – found their way to better-off, middle-class households first. It took quite a long time to reach the point where many of the workers could afford such items. As late as the 1950s, there was still no electricity at Knotts Mill in Watermillock.

New social legislation, as well as a better safety net for those out of work, took the worst edges off the impact of the economic problems for some people. Unemployment benefits for a family of four rose by 240 per cent between 1920 and 1931. All those Liverpool dockers and labourers, whose ranks included several of your forebears and whose lives were made vulnerable by inconsistent and temporary employment opportunities, were among the people aided by the new benefit system. There was progress too in public health, with better treatment, finally, for infectious diseases like tuberculosis. The average life expectancy for women increased in the brief period between the wars by an amazing twenty years. That was largely because new drugs reduced the deadliness of post-natal infections. Women could now realistically hope to see their seventieth birthdays, even if, because of the tyranny of averages (which mean that some people are always unlucky) many still did not.

The position of women improved progressively through the 1920s. Some glass ceilings were broken. In 1919, the first woman MP was elected. Oxford University began to accept women to study for degrees from 1920. In 1922, the first female solicitors, vets and chartered surveyors arrived. The following year London Zoo acquired its first woman curator. In 1927, women for the first time swam across the channel and flew solo across the Irish Sea. On the other hand, women were banned in 1921 from playing football on league grounds.

More legislation inched equality forwards. In 1922 the Law of Property Act equalised inheritance rights between women and men. The following year the Matrimonial Causes Act allowed women to sue for divorce on the grounds of their husband's adultery. And in 1925 the Guardianship of Infants Act gave women and men equal custody rights over their children. Perhaps most important, the expansion of education and better employment opportunities, with a decline in domestic service and more jobs in teaching, nursing and offices, gave many women more control over their own lives. As did the opening in

1921 of Marie Stopes' first clinics offering birth control advice to married women. In 1928 voting rights were finally equalised between men and women. The main reason was that the governing Conservative Party thought many women between the ages of twenty-one and thirty would vote for them.

Women's fashion evolved. For the first time in centuries, short hair, especially the "bob" became common. Make-up, previously found mostly in brothels and theatres, became popular, including lipstick, blusher and mascara. Corsets were out; simple straight cuts, shorter sleeves and higher hemlines were in. Women went out dancing, and to jazz clubs and the cinema and generally seemed to have had a bit more fun. Nevertheless, they almost all still aspired to marriage.

The 1920s was a nicer time to be a child than the previous decade. Children were better nourished, clothed and educated. Child deaths fell. More games and toys permeated, though much fun was still the free sort. Conkers, games of chasing, hide and seek, clapping, running and hopscotch were popular. Marbles, hoops, quoits and spinning tops abounded. The teddy bear, first appearing in 1903, became much more common, as did dolls for girls. And in 1920, Frank Hornby, who had previously invented the Meccano construction toy that was to be a best-seller for more than seventy years, released his first model railway, and quickly opened a large factory to build the sets in Liverpool. Many poorer children, however, had little time for play; they had to run home to do chores or mind younger siblings at the end of the school day. Childhood got a bit longer. By the end of the decade the school leaving age had been increased to fifteen.

The BBC was formed. By the 1920s most of the population were able to listen to the radio. The news and music dominated early broadcasts. The spread of the cinema provided people with a whole new form of entertainment. It grew like topsy, and there were around 4,500 cinemas around the UK before the start of the First World War. Initially, movies were silent, with subtitles and live music played by pianists or organists. Thrillers, dramas and comedies were popular. One of the early stars, Stan Laurel, who appeared in more than a hundred films, was born in Ulverston but his family left for Scotland long before your Lewis or Watson ancestors got there. A lot of the early movies people enjoyed were British, but before long films made in Hollywood were dominating. In the mid-1920s, the first full-colour movies arrived, but it took time before they eclipsed the black-and-white. And in 1929 Alfred Hitchcock released his thriller *Blackmail*, the first British talkie. Popular music evolved, with the development of jazz and ragtime. Smoking and drinking remained major enjoyments: 80 per cent of men and maybe half the women were smokers in the early decades of the century.

Returning from the trenches after the First World War, James Lowcock received a military pension. Many of those who received pensions had been wounded at the front. James bought a plot at the cemetery in St Helens in 1920. It cost him six shillings and eight pence, roughly 33p in today's currency. We can only speculate about why he bought it. What we do know is that he was buried in it on 21 October 1922, at the age of forty. There was a twelve-shilling charge for digging the grave, and a six-shilling payment to the clergyman. His son Jim, just thirteen when his father died, kept the cemetery paperwork, and we still have it. At the time of his death, James Lowcock was living at 18 Volunteer Street. The house – a two-up, two-down terrace very close to the town centre – is still there, just at the end of the street from what is now the YMCA and a spit from St Helens Town Hall.

Having barely finished burying his father, Jim's mother Ada died in 1924. She was just forty-three. Jim was then fifteen. And none of James and Ada Lowcock's children except Jim survived childhood. Ada, born in 1911 and named after her mother, died as an eleven-year-old. Two boys, John and Samuel, were born in 1919 after their father returned from the trenches. But John died in 1927 at the age of eight – he was buried in the same plot as his father, and his elder brother Jim kept the paperwork for that burial too. The undertaker was Herbert Helsby, whose advertising slogan was that they carried out all wedding and funeral arrangements "with smartness and economy". The bill they sent for John's funeral amounted to nearly £6, including the cost of the coffin, the hearse and a coach – and the fee for digging again into the family grave. And then the following year, in October 1928, Samuel also died, was also buried in the family plot, and Jim again kept the paperwork until the end of his life. This time the hearse was a motor car provided by the Cowley Garage, and the price for the funeral was the best part of £7.

So Jim lost his parents, his young sister and two younger brothers, one by one, all in the space of six years. It is hard to imagine the enormity of the impact this must have had on a boy still, by 1928, when his last sibling Samuel died, a teenager himself. He never spoke about what happened. Indeed, the first his children knew of it was when they discovered the burial papers after Jim's own death more than fifty years later in 1984. They were among very few documents – which also included his war records, and a Post Office savings book, which we will come to later – which he kept carefully until he died.

In 1925, at the age of sixteen, and presumably having not long left school, Jim began a four-year apprenticeship as a glass manufacturer with Cannington, Shaw and Co. Ltd, which was part of United Glass Bottle Manufacturers. He was then, as we have said, an orphan, but he was sponsored – young people needed to be recommended for apprenticeships at that time – by Francis Anderson. That was probably his uncle, his mother's brother, rather than his grandfather of the same name. Jim blew glass bottles in the days before that process was automated. The ruined remains of the nineteenth-century factory where he worked and the associated Cannington Shaw Bottle Shop still exist, fenced off but still visible from the car park of the local Tescos in St Helens. There is a Facebook page for the Friends of Cannington Shaw, where you can see pictures of the factory and where other former glass blowers and workers have recorded stories of their working lives. It was a big business – once the largest bottle-making factory in the country, operating 24 hours a day and staffed by 1,200 workers. Women and men worked alongside each other on the automated section of the production line from the early twentieth century, but the women earned a lot less than the men for exactly the same work. If you want to know what your great-grandfather Jim talked and sounded like, watch some of the videos on the Friends of Cannington Shaw Facebook page: there is an uncanny resemblance between what some of the men say and my memories as a young boy of Jim. Cannington Shaw bottles are now collectors' items, found and preserved all over the world and widely marketed across the internet.

Jim lived in and around St Helens all his life: at 53 York Street, 18 Volunteer Street, 47 College Street, 63 French Street and, for most of his life, at the family home he acquired a few years after he married, 3 Honiston Avenue in Rainhill. The houses in Volunteer Street are now festooned with satellite TV dishes. French Street is still there. York Street has gone. College Street, two minutes' walk from Volunteer Street in the town centre, and within easy walking distance of the Cannington Shaw factory, was later redeveloped and is now part of the A571 connecting the town centre with the dual carriageways which link it with Liverpool city centre and the motorways to Scotland and the south.

The Thomas family of Thatto Heath in St Helens made their living as coal miners through the 1920s and 1930s. The miners were at the heart of the events around the General Strike of 1926, one of the best-known episodes of the interwar period. The St Helens District Mines Central Committee represented the interests of 10,000 miners in about a dozen pits across the town. Miners' work was difficult and dangerous. It required them to collaborate and support each other down the pit. That solidarity spread to their organisation above ground too. The men were locked out of their pits for striking on 17 June 1926. Before long 15,000 of them and their supporters marched on the town centre to complain at the inadequacy of poor relief when they and their families had no incomes. A jazz band was established to support and encourage them.

Miners' pay was six shillings (30p) a day in 1914; it increased to nine shillings by 1922, but the value of that was eroded by inflation so they were effectively facing pay cuts. (The Prime Minister, Andrew Bonar Law, was forced to agree these were the facts when questioned in Parliament.) The basic problem was that cheap coal and textiles from elsewhere could now compete with the UK's national output. There was as a result a huge reduction in both cotton and coal exports. In the end, the General Strike failed to increase wages. While for more than fifty years it had been a relatively good option, working as a coal miner now became, compared to other available jobs like factory work and skilled crafts, less well paid. Brian's memory is that:

> "my grandparents' house had none of the modern conveniences – no bathroom, an outside toilet and no central heating or hot water boiler, so after the end of each shift when they all came in black as the Ace of spades they had to wash and bathe in an old tin bath in the living room with water boiled in pans and a kettle over an open coal fire."

No information has survived about Polly Thomas' education or what she did when she left school. Maybe she became one of the many female workers at Cannington Shaw, which could explain how she and Jim met. But that's purely speculation. At this stage we can only guess about her life before she got married. We might find out a little bit more when all the 1921 census records are finally published in January 2022, once the 100-year privacy period ends, which currently restricts access to them. We would also learn more if we were able to look at the 1931 census records. Unfortunately, they were completely destroyed – all of them, for the whole country – in a fire at the Middlesex store in which they were held in 1942.

Pat Connolly went to St Patrick's Roman Catholic School in Griffin Road in Woolwich. More than a hundred years later, it's still there. And some important things about it have not changed. The website now shows boys and girls in bright green jumpers and ties, eyes closed and hands together in prayer, a posture Pat would have been accustomed to. The current mission statement says "prayer and worship are at the heart of all we do" – as they would have been between 1914 and 1920 when Pat was a pupil – especially then, given that pupils and teachers alike would have had a lot of friends and family members at the front. Many of the most fervent prayers must have focused on their safe return. Pat was a regular and committed churchgoer all through his life, as well as a prominent figure in the local church community – including, for example, in his work as a volunteer with the Society of St Vincent de Paul, an organisation we touched on in the opening paragraphs of our story. His Catholicism, inherited from his parents and theirs, was at the heart of his values and behaviour. His headmaster, Mr J Colliston, provided a reference when Pat left school in July 1920, the summer of his fourteenth birthday:

> "Patrick Connolly has been a pupil of the above school for the past six years. During that time he has given satisfaction to his teachers. He has been most regular in his attendance at school and a good worker. I have always found him honest and truthful."

Good worker, reliable, honest and truthful: maybe the things any contemporary employer would have looked for above anything else. Unemployment nationally nearly doubled in the year Pat left school. There was no guarantee of a job. But he was taken on straight away as an apprentice sign writer, the trade he ended up plying, mostly as a small business owner, for the next fifty years. Pat spent most of his working life – though not all of it, as we shall see – in and around Woolwich, Welling and Bexleyheath in south-east London.

Elsie Mock went to school in Welling. Here is what Stella remembers being told of her early life:

> "When she left school she told her mother she wanted to go into service. Her mother told her she would not like it but she said she liked what people wore in service and she did get a job in a household somewhere. Her mother was right. She hated it and only lasted three weeks. She worked in London as a film examiner for 20th Century Fox before she got married. Apparently her boss was very fond of her (much older than her and quite well-off). He wanted to set her up in a florists, he thought it would suit her. She spoke warmly of him but she didn't respond to his advances."

Elsie is the heroine of one of the more curious episodes in the family history of the 1920s, which was captured by local newspapers in south-east London, under headlines like "Welling Burglary: Baker Committed for Trial", "Floury Footprints: Careless Burglar Neatly Caught at Welling" and then the denouement, "Burglar Sentenced: Downfall of a Young Welling Baker". The cast of characters sounds like something out of an Edwardian ripping yarn whose author has overdone the puns: we have a policeman, Detective Batch, the magistrate, one Mr Weigall, the criminal baker, Archibald Ernest Byrne Junior, and then the heroine of the story, Miss Elsie Mock. The tale brims with promise from the outset: the first newspaper report opens with the eye-catching revelation that "An amateur burglar who wore gloves to conceal his finger prints but omitted another elementary precaution appeared before the Dartford magistrates yesterday". This was January 6, just a week after the crime was committed on December 30, so the wheels of justice could move at a fair lick at that time.

The papers reported how the star witness told the court the way the crime was discovered: "Miss Elsie Mock said that on December 29th she was in the front room of the ground floor [*of her home, 3 Albert Place*] when her father closed and fastened the window at 11pm. Next morning at 6.30 she came downstairs and on going into the kitchen found that her brown shoes had been cut up." [*What did the criminal mastermind think that would achieve, one wonders, yet that sadly is never revealed. But let's move on.*] "She missed her grey purse, containing £1 10s in notes and a half crown. On going into the front room she found the bottom half of the window open, and told her parents." [*Her father being Edward Mock, who the journalist curiously renamed Ernest, perhaps knowing he was in the middle of a farce and drawn to recreating an Oscar Wilde play. But I digress...*]

This is perhaps the point to tell you that next door to the Mocks' home, at 1 Albert Place, was a bakers. And, as luck would have it, the sleuth on duty when Elsie later reported to Shooters Hill police station on the morning of 30 December was just the man for the job: the brilliantly named Detective Batch. Who, naturally, rose to the occasion and set straight off in pursuit of the stolen dough. First port of call, as it would be for any officer worth his salt, was the crime scene. As the newspaper account of Batch's evidence at the trial in Gravesend a month later has it, he found when he visited 3 Albert Place "that the front room window had been opened" [*so congratulations to Elsie on having spotted that*]. And, in a new revelation, Detective Batch also discovered that "there were a number of white footprints on the carpet and also on the seat of a leather-topped chair near the window". Lest the casual reader should have missed the import of this vital news, our generous reporter was at hand: "The white marks suggested that the wearer of the boots had been walking in flour". Detective Batch needed no hints of course. [*Though actually he did: the paper reports that it was only "after certain enquiries" that he popped next door to the bakers. What enquiries one wonders? Perhaps it was necessary to ask Elsie or her parents to confirm to the detective that he had indeed walked past a bakers next door on his way into number 3? Or that bakers use flour?*]

On eventually arriving at the bakers, Detective Batch immediately found himself face to face with twenty-five-year-old Archibald Byrne. Upon whom he deployed all his interrogative skills. Told that the detective was inquiring about money and articles stolen from next door, young Archibald had his answer ready: "I know nothing about it." But a detective of Mr Batch's calibre was not to be brushed off quite so easily. As the newspaper reporter told his readers, the detective "noticed some garments hanging from a nail and a lady's purse protruding from one of the pockets. He said to prisoner, 'Is this your purse?' and he said 'Yes'. Where did you get it asked the officer, and the prisoner replied: 'I found it in the lane'." And then our cunning sleuth revealed that the purse "answered the description of one which had been stolen" from next door, and promptly removed young Archibald to the station at Shooters Hill, "pending further enquiries".

There, Elsie identified the purse as hers. And, to continue the newspaper account, "when his finger prints were being taken, prisoner said 'Now she has identified the purse I may as well tell you the truth. I got in there by lifting up the front window.'" [*Yes, I think we've all worked that out by now. Even Detective Batch.*] "I took some notes [*ie bank notes*], two ladies' purses, some silver and a pair of ladies' shoes. The shoes and one of the purses I burnt in the bakehouse fire, so that I should not be found out." [*Hang on a minute, mastermind. You burnt one of the purses and left the other sticking out of a pocket for every passer-by to see?*] "I did not know that I had any flour on my boots. I expect that is what gave me away". [*Er, yes, well, that could have helped. And, thinking it all through again, genius, anything else you might do next time to reduce the chance of being caught?*]

Young Archibald turned out unsurprisingly to have had a bit of a track record of being caught out conducting petty crimes. Magistrate Weigall, weighing it all up, obviously, decided two months as a guest of His Majesty was what the young man needed. But the best bit is saved to the last lines of the final newspaper story: "Mr Weigall ... said that Detective Batch had shown ingenuity and skill in the way he had effected an arrest two days after the burglary had been committed, and also in the manner in which he had conducted the case. He (Mr Weigall) would see that the commendation was brought to the attention of the authorities."

Tom Watson, like his sisters Amy and Clara, went to the Church of England affiliated school in Watermillock. It had originally been established in the 1550s as a grammar school and was rebuilt in the 1860s, initially as a boys' elementary school. A picture from the local newspaper in 1912 shows Tom and his peer group at the school; they were the last boys-only cohort, because girls were admitted shortly after. It appears that after school, Tom trained in Carlisle as an apprentice electrician. There was no work for him close to home. But an American businessman, a Mr Shaw, who owned Halsteads – a Palladian-style mansion on the lakefront at Watermillock, which is now an Outward Bound centre – and knew the family, provided the answer. His interests included a coal mine, the Isabella, in Blyth in Northumberland. You will remember that the Isabella was where John Wilkinson had been killed in 1871. Family lore has it that Mr Shaw was instrumental in getting Tom Watson a job there as an electrician in the 1920s. While working at the Isabella, Tom initially lodged with the Henderson family at number 3 Short Row.

Martin Wilkinson, his wife Mary and their two sons and three daughters lived at number 5 Short Row. (His parents, David and Hannah, were still next door at number 4.) One of his daughters, Mary – who lived to the grand age of ninety-five and was with us when your mum and I got married – recorded her memories of her early life at the Row, and we still have what she wrote. She and her siblings were all born at home (like most babies at the time, generally with no medical involvement). She remembered playing table tennis on a large table in the house as a child. She also recalled:

> "It was so crowded and I can't remember where we all slept. There were two double beds in each bedroom and [*babies slept*] in the sideboard in the sitting room....Poor Mother must have made everyone welcome but how did she cook for everyone?

The Bella still has a soft spot in my heart even though I wouldn't want all the hardships like what Mother had to endure...

The other day one of the ladies here [*in her retirement home*] was talking about using newspaper in the toilet and it was surprising how many of us remembered it. I still remember scrubbing the toilet seat. Can you remember the wash houses now called laundries?!"

Yes, I rather think all that would stick in the memory. (The outdoor wash houses combined the communal toilets and a space with running water for washing, including for clothes.)

Martin's daughter Florrie and her siblings went to Newsham infants and junior school, a short walk from the mine. Her two sisters, Mary and Nance, passed the entrance test for grammar school, but on a miner's pay there was no way Martin could afford the fees, and there was no scholarship available. Employment opportunities for girls leaving school were limited, but there was a regular demand for shop assistants and the Wilkinson sisters all found work in local branches of retail chain stores. The Wilkinsons were, Bill recalls, "devout High-Church Anglicans, incense included".

Mary Rudd went to school in Liverpool and from there to work in a factory. Her parents, Richard and Sarah, still had two rooms in the tenement at Ashfield Cottages. Sarah would sit on the landing in her black dress, black apron and black hair tied up, a friendly, jolly and generous person. Richard still sought work in the docks, which was not easy in the 1920s and 1930s, but they managed to cope and he put a brave face on things, never outwardly downbeat. Richard was neat and dapper in his three-piece suit, and he enjoyed a smoke and the newspaper. His grandchildren remember him, a short, stocky and voluble man, sitting in front of the coke-fuelled range and chatting to all visitors. The dust and smoke from the coke range blackened the atmosphere – one of the reasons most people wore dark clothes was to conceal the dirt, marks and smudges whatever they wore inevitably acquired. Sarah later became diabetic but would send her grandchildren down to the shops to buy her biscuits. They were pillars of the local Catholic church, and the priests were frequent visitors to Ashfield Cottages.

Peter Lewis, a bright boy, was another of those who passed the exam to win a place at secondary school when he was about eleven. But like the Wilkinsons in Blyth, his parents, still living in the tenements, could not afford to send him. His mother Julia was a gregarious, kind-hearted, outgoing person, taking in and bringing up orphaned children. She was organised, infinitely patient and what would today be described as an excellent networker. The church was the centre of their lives too; there were statues depicting the Sacred Heart of Mary and other Catholic icons all over the house, and Julia would regularly cook for the half dozen priests at the local presbytery. She organised parties, cooked for the wider family and liked the cinema and the pub. Charles, her husband, was said to be a "home devil and a street angel". Outgoing and entertaining in the pub, with an ear for music, he was jealous and a bit domineering of his wife. He is said on one occasion to have requested a public announcement at the cinema asking her to leave the show to attend to matters at home. (She knew how to get her own back: when he was out Julia's sisters would bring Guinness and choc ices round and they would party among themselves.) The mid-1920s were not a good time for a young person to try to find a job in Liverpool, but Peter managed to find work as a uniformed bell boy in one of the city's big hotels. He was close to his mother, supporting her financially including by buying her clothes – some of which she daren't wear for fear of winding up her husband. Peter was also a keen cyclist and camper.

———·———

The early adult years of your great-grandparents – the ninth generation – through the 1920s saw the first arrival of many things we are familiar with today but that had not existed before: Kellogg's cornflakes, Mars Bars, shops like Sainsbury's and Marks & Spencer becoming chains across the country, seaside holiday camps, organic food, paperbacks, skiing, semi-detached houses, mortgages, roadside garages, gyms, nightclubs and the Hanky-Panky cocktail. (Not familiar with that one? Gin, sweet vermouth and a dash of Fernet-Branca, a bitter herbal liqueur.) As electricity became more widespread, the first properly working electric kettle was marketed in 1923, and electronic adverts arrived in Piccadilly Circus the following year, though they were light years from the neon blazes of today.

Many aspects of this era, though, were rather more grim. A visiting American professor of English saw "rows upon rows of identical grey houses where strident women with untidy babies stand in doorways … the smell of cheap petrol, fish and chips, smoke and wet woollens; tree-less streets; advertisements for Lyons' tea, Capstan and Woodbine cigarettes; miserable shops displaying through their unwashed windows pink rock candy, drill overalls, tinned sardines, sticky kippers, sucking dummies for babies, garish underwear, impossible hats ...". She was mentally drawing a contrast with prosperous, leafy, US college towns. And it's worth remembering that even her gloomy depiction had features that would have looked attractive fifty years earlier to residents of the streets she described now.

People still rarely travelled far from home except for a holiday, often at the nearest seaside resort. Only the rich (or those wearing a uniform and carrying a rifle across their shoulder) ever left the country. And while pretty much everyone had seen a car, most had not been in one and only a small minority owned them. The car industry was gradually established during the first decades of the twentieth century. Powered public transport – buses, trams and the underground – gradually got the horses off the streets.

We have so far in this chapter described your great-grandparents' lives in the 1920s, when they completed their schooling and started work and apprenticeships. We are moving on now to the 1930s. As far as we can tell from the stories passed down the family and the other records we have, during the 1920s most of your great-grandparents would have been able to enjoy the benefits of growing incomes, relatively few responsibilities and the progressive dissemination of lots of time-saving and life-enhancing new technologies. Electricity! The cinema! They also had more leisure and other opportunities than their own parents experienced as young adults. In the 1930s their lives were further enhanced by marriage, children and material progress. We will move on to all that now.

But first it is important to recognise that the period from 1929 to 1933 was one of enormous stress and hardship across the country as a whole (and in most of the rest of the world). Even if your great-grandparents were able to weather the storm a little better than some, as seems to have been the case, they cannot but have been affected by the troubling background conditions. Because this was the time of the Wall Street Crash, the Great Depression and mass unemployment.

The British economy – and especially jobs – were still excessively dominated by the old industries of coal, iron, textiles and shipbuilding. The UK was becoming less competitive in all of them. That was especially true in the north-west and the north-east. Those regions were particularly hard hit by the slump. By whatever mix of luck and judgement, most of your great-grandparents found their way into some of the safer and better-paid new industries: engineering, electrics, glass and film. But there were opportunities in other areas too, including artificial textiles (rayon, nylon and the rest, which were thought very exciting for decades even if they are looked down on now), chemicals, food processing and packaging and motor vehicles. Women especially seemed to have found their way into newer industries, though some, as we have seen, still flirted with domestic service on the way.

Avoiding unemployment was the difference between a decent life and a really tough one. While many people could get unemployment benefits, they were too mean to live on with any decency. Many of the working-class poor who dipped in and out of work were hungry, badly fed, badly clothed and badly housed through the 1930s. One consequence was a slowing down of the improvement in child survival that had been a feature of the twentieth century up to then. Life's lottery determined a lot. As William Beveridge, the prominent social reformer, wrote, "there is not a special class or kind of people who constitute the unemployed. They come from almost every calling and have as great a variety of interests and capacities as any other member of the community. They are ordinary decent people to whom an extraordinary misfortune has happened."

And there were a lot of them: three and a half million in 1932, concentrated especially in the northern heartlands of the old industries. Unemployment also brought boredom. Some tried their hands at allotments, a carryover from the war; others found solace in the warmth of local libraries, "a winter garden of rest", but beware of falling asleep, because that would lead to the formidable, mostly female, librarians throwing you out; others still joined social clubs, like the 150 set up in the empty shops and basements of Liverpool, where you could play billiards or cards.

It took a long time, but housing improved hugely between the wars. From 1919 to 1937, twelve million people, nearly 30 per cent of the population, were rehoused. The Connollys and the Lowcocks were among them. Local authorities built many new houses, renting them out to local families. One of the problems was what people could afford to pay in rent, which was often insufficient. In order to help address that, local authorities started subsidising rent according to family circumstances: less to pay if incomes were lower or there were more children in the household. That helped get poorer families into better accommodation than they would otherwise have had. Three quarters of the new homes were private, bought with mortgages by people like the Connollys in south-east London. Greater London was growing by three quarters of a million people a year in the mid-1930s. They all needed somewhere to live. A wage or salary of £4 a week was enough for a mortgage and many people had one. The required deposit fell from 25 per cent to maybe just 5 per cent. Ads appeared: "Why pay rent when you can own your own home?". New houses had electricity and running water. Overall, two thirds of households were wired up by 1939 – including many, like the Wilkinsons, who had not yet moved into new homes. It's easy to forget that almost no-one had electricity at home forty years earlier. Better houses also needed better furnishing – good news for joiners like the Watsons. And decorating: many people liked prints of the old masters like Turner and Constable (and some of us still have them).

Fewer and fewer people lived in rural areas: just six million of a population now of more than forty million. In 1938, only half the rural parishes had sewage systems, 90 per cent of farms had no electricity and a third of parishes had no piped water. Rural pay was bad. Farmworkers left for factory jobs – in the case of Oxfordshire, frequently for the Cowley car factories – partly in search of the better housing, water and electricity in the towns and cities. Agricultural productivity improved with more use of tractors and larger farms. But one consequence of the departure of rural workers was that there was less cultivation of arable land, and dependence on imported food reached 70 per cent. That had to be urgently reversed from 1939 when war and a potential blockade threatened the nation with starvation.

There were just 100,000 cars on British roads in 1918. Car prices fell by half between 1924 and 1936. More people could afford them. By the start of the Second World War, the number had grown to two million, though many were commercial or military and other public vehicles. By comparison, we now have thirty-three million cars on the roads. Most people were still reliant on more traditional forms of getting around. This is what Brian remembers from Rainhill in the 1940s:

"Very few people could afford a car and the usual form of transport was bicycle or bus. Horse and cart was the transport still of the local tradespeople, milkman, baker, grocer and coal merchant. I remember breaking my arm playing football and being transported to the local hospital on the back of the milkman's float, which did not have pneumatic tires and travelled over cobblestones. That was the worst journey of my life."

In 1930 the speed limit of 20 mph was abolished. That was rapidly followed by a big increase in accidents. So in 1934 the speed limit was brought back, this time at 30 mph. And, to protect the innocent, drivers were now required to have third-party insurance. The arrival of cars did not bring many more roads; dual carriageways and motorways were to come much later.

It would be some years before anyone in the family could afford to buy one, but Tom Watson – who was a bit of a mechanical and electrical genius – built a car for himself in the late 1920s or early 1930s. Starting with a motorbike engine, he designed and assembled an open-topped, tandem-configuration four-wheeler, with a big steering wheel, a glass windscreen and a hand-pumped horn in the place of the wing mirror. He drove it and took passengers – including his father. How long it lasted and what happened to it is a mystery, which is a pity because it was quite an achievement. There is no evidence or memory of it being a feature of his years in Blyth.

The 1930s also saw the arrival of commercial air travel, but it was long into the future before any of your great-grandparents or their children first went on a plane. It was still the case that hardly anyone outside the richest elites ever left the country. But at home, travel and days out became more frequent. The Ramblers Association was founded in 1935. This was the peak era for the bike, a relatively cheap form of transport many people could now afford. You could get a new model Raleigh for five shillings a week on "deferred terms". The number of cyclists doubled in the five years after 1929, reaching more than ten million. The Cyclists Touring Club did all road users a favour by lobbying for potholes to be filled in and roads to be properly tarred. In general, though, people did not exercise much. In 1935 more than 90 per cent of boys between fourteen and eighteen did no physical activity. Newcastle, apparently, was particularly immobile. Sun worshipping grew in popularity. Though that was also difficult in Newcastle.

The cinema was the dominant popular pastime. More than 900 million cinema tickets were sold in the UK in 1934, and the numbers grew further through the decade. The most famous man on earth in the early 1930s was Charlie Chaplin. Born to an alcoholic father in Lambeth, he was performing in music halls from the age of nine, an orphan at fourteen and then moved to Hollywood where he made a string of world-beating movies. Every two-bit town had a cinema, and the larger cities had newly built "picture palaces", huge structures dwarfing the grubby streets in which they were located. Liverpool had nearly a hundred cinemas. Their comfortable interiors and plush seats were mostly occupied by women. Unaccompanied women could go to the flicks in a way they could not go to the pub without being frowned upon; a mother could take in a matinee before the children came home from school and she had to prepare the family meal (though not always, as Julia Lewis had found, without being disturbed). There were musical interludes in the programme. Between films, the curtains would close across the screen, an organ would rise up from the well of the cinema and the player, some of whom became household names in their own right, would offer a ten-minute recital of popular songs and tunes. People would watch whatever was being shown. Historical dramas were popular, including ones about Henry VIII and Queen Victoria. But Walt Disney's first full-length, gloriously colourful cartoon, *Snow White and the Seven Dwarfs*, released in 1938 and seen by 28 million people across the country, was the hit of the decade. Disney's wife had warned him off it: "No-one's ever gonna pay a dime to see a dwarf picture."

Beach holidays reached a new peak of popularity in the 1930s. This was the era in which people on beaches started to look like us. Until the 1930s men were not permitted to wear bathing costumes which let their chests be seen, except on Brighton beach, which has always been ahead of the times. A few women started to wear costumes that left their arms, shoulders and most of their legs bare. But the bikini was not invented until 1946. And the vast majority of people still wore their formal suits, long dresses and heavy coats sitting on the sands.

Seaside resorts all round the country were booming, even in some pretty inclement places. This was the high point of the knickerbocker glory (forgotten now, though remembered in my childhood, not that I was ever allowed one), Punch and Judy, the band on the promenade, seaside photographers, saucy postcards, donkeys, tin whistles and sand castles. Blackpool outdid everywhere else: parks, the

Winter Gardens, seven miles of (occasionally) sun-kissed golden sand and more fish and chips than you can imagine. Those were just the tasteful elements. Then there were the freak shows: the "ugliest woman on earth" (a thirty-three-stone Irish woman with jagged teeth), a three-legged boy and a five-legged cow. Even more bizarre were the "starving brides", emaciated women on display wearing wedding dresses who were offered £250 if they fasted for a month sustained only by two pints of water a day.

This was also a good time for the Lake District tourist industry. People came to follow the footsteps of Wordsworth and Coleridge, the poets they learned at school, and to see where Peter Rabbit and Beatrix Potter's other popular fictional animals had come from. They also wanted to look at the settings of Arthur Ransome's best-selling *Swallows and Amazons* books. They were written in Windermere, where Ransome sought refuge with his wife, who had been Trotsky's secretary, when they both concluded the Russian revolution was getting a little too hot. Coach trips round the Lakes brought lots of people in during the 1930s. Many of them certainly dropped by the Brackenrigg Inn.

Birth rates continued to fall. By 1940, only 30 per cent of families had three or more children (most of your great-grandparents were among the 30 per cent, as we shall see). The two-child family was becoming the norm. Infant mortality fell by 70 per cent between 1901 and 1935, and parents were increasingly confident that all their children would survive. Access to good-quality family planning was still far from universal though, and many people were stuck with the oldest methods of regulating their family size, including, in tragically too many cases, the most dangerous back street ones.

Most working-class women were still having their babies at home in the 1930s, possibly but not always with the help of a midwife. The better off often gave birth in private nursing homes. From 1936 the Midwives Act obliged local authorities to provide trained midwives, but only from 1946 did hospital births exceed those at home. Before the Second World War, families had to pay out of their own pockets for whatever service they got, because married women were not covered by the national health insurance scheme. Women's health accordingly was often worse than men's. They suffered varicose veins, anaemia, haemorrhoids, rheumatism and arthritis, all made worse for many by simple exhaustion. The problem was not made any better by the shortage of female health workers. Women often did not want to see a male doctor.

Doctors in any case still had little to offer: aspirin, kaolin (used to treat diarrhoea) and morphine might have been the limit of the drugs; a stethoscope, thermometer, ear syringe and maybe a speculum the limit of the kit. There were some improvements. Sulphonamide drugs to treat puerperal fever significantly reduced maternal mortality. And greater understanding of the importance of vitamins led to the wider use of vitamins C and D to stave off scurvy and rickets. It is important not to put too gloomy a complexion on all this. Despite everything, life expectancy increased from around fifty in 1900 to sixty in the 1930s.

Hat wearing declined as the decade progressed. Underwear got lighter. Women's corsets and stays could weigh seven pounds, apparently, so not only could they not bend over, they could barely stand up either. It's hard to imagine any of the wearers were sorry to see them go. But not all changes of dress were for the better. That horror-show of a garment, the man's cardigan, became fashionable.

Chain stores sold clothes and started setting the fashion tone, sometimes taking their lead from members of the royal family who had always prided themselves on being natty dressers. Burtons had more than 550 shops across the country by 1939. Freeman Hardy and Willis (shoes), Austin Reed, British Home Stores and the ubiquitous Co-Op spread too. Fur was popular, and fox numbers declined as a result. (They have recovered.) In 1935 *Good Housekeeping* magazine, which even then was not exactly at the forefront of cultural innovation, reported that its typical town-dwelling reader was spending £15 a year (equivalent to a small fortune now) on make-up, hair-dos and manicures.

A lot of shopping was done through hire purchase (HP), conceptually the predecessor to credit cards. But, in a revealing insight into what had still not changed, married women were not allowed to sign HP agreements without their husbands' consent. High streets, which had historically been dominated by single-proprietor-owned stores, all started to look the same. Every one had a Woolworths, a Boots, a Greggs, a Lyons and a United Dairy as well as a couple of bookshops, a chemist or two, and several fruit and veg shops and tobacconists. Florrie Wilkinson and her sisters were among the huge numbers of women who found jobs in retail chains: Mary and Nance with the Co-Op, and Florrie with Walter Willson's, a grocery chain whose shop fronts (there were more than a hundred of them across the north, including in Ulverston) advertised that they were "one of the branches of a colossal business".

The 1930s was the era in which people in the elite classes most flirted with political extremism ranging from communism to fascism. It is notable that radical ideologies attracted little interest from the great majority of working people who, now they had the opportunity, consistently used their votes to support moderate political parties. One other indicator of the declining fortunes of the super-rich was in their houses. Some 7 per cent of the great country houses were demolished between the wars. Others were converted into schools (one of which became mine) and others still sold off or given away to the National Trust. A lot of this was the result of progressive taxation and laws that incentivised those among the rich who could not afford death duties to hand over their houses in exchange for being allowed to keep living in parts of them.

When asked, most Britons in the 1930s said they were Christian, before adding "but of course I'm not religious". People thought it was a good idea for children to be given religious education at school, and 70 per cent of babies were baptised. Notionally, 60 per cent of the population were Church of England, and about 5 per cent Catholic. But the Catholics – not least those in and around Liverpool, but elsewhere too – were more fervent, attended more services and frequently brought new recruits in when they married, an example of which we shall see shortly. For many others, church was social and to instil values rather than religion. The BBC originally did not broadcast on Sunday mornings and evenings to avoid being accused of keeping people out of the pews; they gave that up when it became clear that people were simply switching to independent radio stations broadcasting from the Continent.

By the end of the decade, 98 per cent of the population could receive one BBC radio channel, and 85 per cent could get two. The Corporation had become the largest employer of musicians in the country. Sports broadcasting had begun, with live reporting on the Grand National and the FA Cup from 1927. By 1934, the BBC was broadcasting whole afternoons of sports commentaries. The football results were listened to with great attention, partly because something like a quarter of the population were betting £50 million a season on the pools, trying to predict the elusive list of eight or so games each week that would result in draws and so win the jackpot. Filling in the coupon became an activity for much of the family in households across the country. While television had started, hardly anything was broadcast, almost no-one was close enough to the transmitters to receive it and about the same number could afford a set.

———·———

We now finally reach the point at which the tenth generation, your grandparents, enter the story. Your great-grandparents all married within a few years of each other, during the 1930s. And they soon started their families.

Tom Watson and Florence Wilkinson got married in Blyth in the last weeks of 1931. Florrie's sister Mary, then fourteen, was a bridesmaid. She recalled that the wedding was "early in the morning as lots of weddings were then and they went to Watermillock later in the day for their honeymoon".

Tom was during the 1930s working for the United Bus Company in Newcastle. He and Florrie had a flat in West Jesmond on the outskirts of the city. For some years there were no children. Florrie miscarried a son almost at full term. Mary told Bill years later "we were all so sad and rejoiced when you were safely delivered". Bill was born in 1938, at the Royal Victorian Infirmary, Newcastle's main city hospital. Tom was then thirty-four and they had been married for seven years. It was not just on the Wilkinson side of the family that there was rejoicing. Unlike the Wilkinsons, the Watsons of Watermillock had no grandchildren. Tom was the only one of their six original children to have married. One imagines that news of Bill's arrival was therefore keenly awaited. It was conveyed by telephone from Newcastle to the Brackenrigg Inn, and from there a messenger ran down the road to Knotts Mill. The elder Tom, who liked a pint, is said to have greeted the news that he was now a grandfather by accompanying the messenger back to the Brackenrigg Inn where he stood a round or more of drinks.

Pat Connolly and Elsie Mock were married at St Stephen's Catholic Church in Belle Grove, Welling on 17 June 1933. She was still a film examiner, living round the corner on Belle Grove Road; he was still living with his parents at 20 Heverham Road in Plumstead. Elsie's father Edward was still working at the arms factory in Woolwich, and Pat's father Jack was still at St Nicholas' infirmary. In order to marry Pat, Elsie had to take instruction from his parish priest and become a Catholic. (Father Clifford Nevatt, who became a long-lasting family friend, was the parish priest at St Stephen's for more than thirty years until his death in 1961. Initially rejected for the seminary, he tried his hand at insurance and then monastic life, neither of which satisfied him. When he did eventually become a priest he was a good one: well known by Pat and Elsie's children and always well regarded.) Elsie had also, of course, given up her older admirer, whose employ she left when she got married. There were no hard feelings. She told your grandmother Stella he gave her "a very nice present, a canteen of cutlery from Mappin and Webb".

Pat and Elsie were quite the dashing young couple. Photos of her in her best outfit depict the iconic interwar young woman: slim, short bobbed hair, modern calf-length dress, fashionable shoes with a prominent heel, a single strap and partially exposed foot. He was smart, confident, bespectacled and bestowed of a fine head of thick, wavy brown hair (which he kindly later passed on, via his daughter, to me, though I don't have it anymore). They spent part of their courtship riding a tandem round the countryside. That was a common wooing gambit at the time. Tales of their escapades, focused around who was supposed to apply the brakes, and the consequences when they (meaning he) did not, reverberated around the family – both children and grandchildren – for decades. The experience clearly made a deep impression on her, and he never fully lived it down. Pat was always a bit of a joker. He liked entertaining, inheriting his father's thespian genes, and had business cards printed as "Pat Connolly the Original Eccentric Dancer", offering performances at "ballrooms, concerts, theatres etc". Years later he developed a magician's act with which he entertained the grandchildren.

Pat was now established as a successful self-employed sign writer. He was good at it, and popular with his clients. A Mr Tricker (his real name, apparently), the director of one of them, Mackintosh Brothers, who described themselves on their letterhead as "high class mineral water manufacturers" wrote of Pat that "he is the finest sign writer in south London" and advised others "Leave it to Pat, he will make a good job of it". A few years later, another, Bonners of Welling, near neighbours of the Connollys when they lived at Upper Wickham Lane in Welling, "highly recommended" Pat's "thorough workmanship" in the coach and sign writing trades. Bonners were a removal company and commented that "our furniture pantechnicons" (old fashioned word for lorry), painted with the company name by Pat, were "well known all over the country for their good appearance". Pat did the signs on vehicles, shop fronts, banks, town halls and other public buildings. He once had a commission to redo the gold leaf on the statue of the woman bearing the scales of justice which sits atop the Old Bailey courthouse, one of the emblematic sculptures of London. Towards the end of his working life he emblazoned the 006 Hovercraft launched in the sea off Kent in May 1969, a venture which unfortunately did not work out as well as all its instigators had hoped.

Pat made a decent living, and Elsie (who much later had a job as a civil service clerk in an office in south-east London) was soon a mother. Two girls, Maureen and Carole, arrived and then in 1940 Stella, who later had a brother, John, and a younger sister, Sue. Elsie also had an earlier son who had not survived. The family were among those who were able to take advantage of the burgeoning mortgage industry, and Pat and Elsie bought and sold a series of houses in and around Welling from the 1930s through to the early 1950s: Lancelot Road, Faraday Road and Upper Wickham Lane, all within easy walking distance of each other, and of the church and the Catholic primary school.

A week after Pat and Elsie's wedding, and 200 miles away, Jim Lowcock married Polly Thomas in St Helens. Jim earned a good wage as a glass blower. They initially lived in a small house in French Street in St Helens. But a few years after marrying, needing more room for a larger family, they moved into a bigger, newly built rented house at Honiston Avenue, in Rainhill, outside the town centre. On 10 May 1933, just before getting married, Jim had withdrawn £90 (thousands of pounds in today's money) from his Post Office savings account. He no doubt used it to pay for the wedding and setting up home. Honiston Avenue had two rooms downstairs. By the entrance hall there was a front room which, as was the tradition at the time, was kept for best and almost never used. Behind that was a parlour which also served as the kitchen and had a cooker. Years later, a glass-fronted lean-to conservatory was added at the back, and that became the kitchen. I remember as a little boy Polly toasting bread for me under the gas grill in the lean-to as we watched Jim in his greenhouse and mused over what all the pottering would amount to. (A handful of tomatoes months later, normally.) Upstairs there were three small bedrooms and a bathroom.

Jim spent nearly ten years as a part-time soldier in the Territorial Army from the late 1920s, and was also a roller-skating dance champion and a Sunday school teacher. He and Polly may perhaps have met through the church (though we guessed about other possibilities, too, earlier). The Thomas family remained miners, with Polly's brothers following their father into the pit in Thatto Heath. The youngest son, who Brian says was the brightest, became a mine overseer – effectively the underground manager:

> "The older brothers and even his father were effectively therefore obliged to do what he told them to do and I remember many contra-temps within the family with particularly my grandfather saying he wasn't going to bloody do what his son wanted him to do!"

In December 1933, Polly gave birth to her first child, Mavis. In May 1935 Brian came along. In 1942, just before Jim left the country to fight in the war, Colin was born. And then, after the war, in 1947, Sandra. None of the names Jim and Polly gave their children had ever, as far as I can tell, been in the family before. That was, as you have seen, a marked departure from what had happened in previous generations. It is almost as though they wanted to turn over a whole new page.

Peter Lewis and Mary Rudd married in Liverpool in 1937. They were both committed and active Catholics, as they remained throughout their lives. Peter had always managed to find work and was by then working in one of the fast-growing new industries, for an electrical supplies company called Ashleys Electricals, which made light switches, sockets and the like. Peter and Mary's first child, Marie, was born in a hospital in the Sefton district of Liverpool in January 1939. The authorities, seeing that war was coming, started relocating strategic industries. And so, after a hundred years in the city – longer for some branches of the family – the Lewises left Liverpool. Ashleys moved in April 1939 to the southern Lake District town of Ulverston.

Down the road from the shipbuilding town of Barrow, forty-five minutes from the centre of the Lake District in Windermere and positioned with views over Morecambe Bay (which was linked to the town centre by a canal), Ulverston was, before the arrival of light industry, a quiet market town. The settlement was recorded in the Domesday Book, the name originating in a Norse family name meaning wolf warrior (which explains the presence of a wolf on the town's coat of arms). Over the centuries it housed monasteries, survived as a trade route and, in the seventeenth century, when Balthasar Mock arrived in Barnstaple and the Lowcocks were in Skipton, became the birthplace of the Quaker movement when George Fox set up shop at Swarthmoor Hall. A grammar school was established late in the seventeenth century. There was a modest chemical industry from the beginning of the twentieth century, with Sadler's Chemical Works using the by-products from other local industries to produce the preferred fertiliser for turnip growers. The arrival of Ashleys, then Armstrong Siddley and after the war the Glaxo conglomerate gave Ulverston a boost but did not change its essence.

Peter, Mary and baby Marie were initially put up in bed and breakfasts but soon moved into a modern, newly built three-bedroom house with a kitchen, bathroom and a garden. Their street, The Ellers, was near the centre of the town and walking distance to the factory. Peter, a city boy, liked exploring the Lakes on foot and by bike, and the family enjoyed weekend days at the beach in Ulverston. As they had been in Liverpool, Peter and Mary were prominent in the church community. He was a regular at the Catholic men's club, enjoying billiards, snooker and a pint with his friends. He and Mary also went to ballroom dancing classes. Ashley's proved a good employer in a good business and Peter spent the rest of his working life there, largely as the foreman on his shift on the factory floor. They brought up their five children – Marie, Richard, Annie, Sheila and later Stephen – in the town, and enjoyed their retirements there too.

But that was a long way off. As soon as they arrived in Ulverston, it was clear that the immediate challenge was simply to survive what was about to be unleashed.

7

Survival and Recovery:
The 1940s

---

in which your grandparents (and their parents)
survive the Second World War and its aftermath,
and get an education.

E veryone heard that war had been declared via the
BBC. Nearly nine million radio licences were sold in
1938. Air raids were expected, and there were sirens
immediately. The government had circulated leaflets before
war was declared on what to do: go to public shelters, cellars
or vaults. One and a half million corrugated iron Anderson
shelters had been distributed for people to put up in their
gardens. Neighbours of the Lewises had one. So did the
Wilkinsons in Blyth. Bill's memory is that it was "damp,
creepy, candle-lit and claustrophobic, especially when
wearing a gas mask". Everyone had a gas mask to protect
them against what was the biggest fear, that chlorine gas
bombs would be dropped, as they had been against soldiers
in the First World War. People were encouraged to practise
wearing their masks for fifteen minutes a day so they were
ready when they were needed. They never were.

Just as had been the case for your great-grandparents a generation earlier, the Second World War dominated your grandparents' childhoods. It was the overwhelming fact, pervasive in every single dimension of the lives of the tenth generation for nearly six years. Brian was born in 1935; Bill in 1938; Marie in 1939; and Stella in 1940. So they all have at least some wartime memories, though a small child's perspective was not the same as that of their parents.

A huge evacuation programme began on 1 September 1939, focused mostly on moving children from the most impoverished inner cities which were thought vulnerable to bombing. In the largest mass movement in the country's history, a million and a half people were relocated in the first three days of September. The programme was voluntary but the authorities had ways of signalling what they wanted to happen. The Liverpool *Daily Post* spoke of the risk of 300,000 casualties a week when hostilities began, a clear hint that people ought to leave the city in their own interest while they had the chance. The Lewis family were safe in Ulverston, though Barrow just down the road was to come under attack from the bombers. Newcastle was known to be a potential target, and Florrie took baby Bill to the Lake District to stay with his father's family. Tom stayed behind. In total between half and three quarters of the children in Liverpool and Newcastle left. Many schools closed, giving the doubters another nudge. The Lowcock family stayed in St Helens, as did the Connollys in Welling. The evacuation was, however, short-lived. By January 1940 many of the evacuees had gone back home. There had so far been no bombing, and many people decided it was better to stick it out in the places they knew rather than unfamiliar countryside locations where they were often reliant on the kindness of strangers. Not everyone returned home: Florrie kept Bill in the Lake District.

The gloom was real as well as metaphorical. Electricity companies cut the voltage to save power, so even rooms which had electric lighting were dim. A blackout was enforced to prevent the bombers navigating by the lights of towns and cities across the country. It was monitored by air raid wardens and policemen, and people could be prosecuted for failing to comply. One of the main consequences was that people who had to go out at night floundered around dangerously in the dark. There was a big increase in death on the roads, with cyclists especially vulnerable. The regulations were soon amended to allow traffic to shine a sliver of light onto the road ahead to reduce the rate of accidents.

When the Blitz began in September 1940, the damage was dramatic and widespread. The bombing was all at night, when it was easier for the attacking planes to avoid the anti-aircraft guns. Hundreds of bombers and fighter planes attacked night after night for the best part of nine months. From the outset, the industrial centres, including London, Liverpool and Newcastle, bore the brunt. By December 1940 London had been attacked 120 times and Liverpool sixty; and more than a hundred other towns and cities had been hit at least once. In Liverpool the famous Lewis's department store, the Central Library, churches, schools and hospitals were all damaged, as well as the docks and the Tate & Lyle sugar factory. Merseyside was raided on seven successive nights in May 1941. For a few days at one point many people marched miles each night out into the countryside for safety, returning the following morning.

Polly Thomas and Jim Lowcock,
ninth generation, St Helens,
circa 1930.

Brian, tenth generation, Polly, Colin and Mavis Lowcock,
St Helens, 1943, a picture taken to send to Jim who was away
fighting with the Allies in north Africa.

Pat, Maureen and Carole Connolly (and Pat's new car)
at Lancelot Road, Welling, 1938.

Police Constable Pat Connolly,
Welling, circa 1941.

Maureen, John,
Carole and Stella Connolly,
tenth generation,
Welling, January 1944.

(Back row l–r) Florence Watson, Nance Wilkinson, Mary Pearson (eighth generation), Nan Watson (ninth generation); (front row l–r) Amy Watson (ninth generation), Martin Wilkinson (eighth generation), Bill Watson (tenth generation) and Mary Wilkinson, Old Church Bay, Ullswater, 1941.

Tom and Bill, Old Church Bay, 1941.

Tom the elder and Bill, Knotts Sawmill, 1940.

St Ann's Parish Church choir, Rainhill, circa 1945. Brian is in the middle of the front pew. His future brother-in-law, Norman Pridham (partially obscured), is second from left on the third row of choristers from the front.

Polly, Sandra, Brian, Colin and Jim, circa 1954.

National Service: Private Lowcock, Royal Signals, 1953.

RMS Strathaird, which took the Connollys to Australia in 1956.
Their cabin is marked by a barely visible 'X'.

Stella on the Triumph Roadster, 1959.

Marie Lewis, tenth generation, Ulverston, circa 1959.

Brian the accountant.

Bill the graduate.

*Four generations 1969: The author is in the middle of the children,
flanked on his right by brothers, first, Nick, and second, Paul;
and on his left by cousins Christopher and Jeremy Pridham
(all eleventh generation). The adults are (l-r) Brian, Stella,
Norman, Mavis, Max Ratoff and Sandra, John Thomas
(eighth generation), Polly, Jim and Colin.*

*Four more generations 2000: Mary (Rudd), Julia Watson
(eleventh generation), Helena Lowcock (twelfth generation)
and Marie (Lewis).*

At the height of the attacks, some people were relocated. Peter and Mary Lewis' parents and several of their siblings got on a train north heading for Ulverston; the train only made it part of the way and they had to walk the final stretch. They moved in with friends and family: Peter's parents into the front room of his young family's new house, and the Rudds into the sitting room of the house next door. Everyone originally on the street was from Liverpool, since they had moved together with Ashleys, and the new influx recreated the tight-knit, cramped conditions they had all known in the city. But they got on with it. Charles Lewis found work as a drayman – carrying beer round the town's pubs by horse and cart. (The by-products of that form of transport were the same as they had always been, obviously, but now Peter Lewis would follow the cart round town with a bucket and shovel and capture the manure for his roses.) The aerospace and motor manufacture firm Armstrong Siddley set up shop servicing aircraft engines by the side of the canal in Ulverston, and several of the Lewis and Rudd siblings worked there. Some of these businesses returned to Liverpool after the war, and many members of the Lewis and Rudd clans went back with them. But Ashleys stayed, so Peter and Mary and their family did too.

After the war, the Germans' bombing maps for St Helens were found, with lines drawn around the industrial facilities. In the nine months of the most intense bombing, from August 1940, 43,000 civilians were killed and two million made homeless. By the end of the war, four million of the twelve million homes in the country had been damaged, as well as one in five of the schools and hospitals. Air raids were exhausting as well as destructive, with people spending night after night in ill-equipped and uncomfortable – but safer – shelters. They got used to it remarkably quickly, and before long it was the weather that depressed people more than the bombers. As one diary writer recorded, "One is relieved to find how little bombs can do as compared with the mental picture one had." In reality, though, while casualties were not as high as the government planners had feared, the physical damage was huge and was to take decades to repair. The Wilkinsons in Blyth had a piece of shrapnel through the bedroom ceiling, either from a bomb or from an anti-aircraft shell. It was prominently displayed on the mantelpiece in the front room for years afterwards.

The air raids largely fizzled out in mid-1941, as Hitler focused his attentions elsewhere. There were in 1943 a spate of attacks on some of the country's most ancient cities, at least partly in retaliation to the bombing of German cities. The Germans chose the targets from travel guides, picking out Bath, York, Exeter and Norwich. Then there was a renewed threat in the last phase of the war with V1 rockets fired across the Channel. They were deadly and accurate, and aimed at central London, where the potential for destroying important or popular buildings and therefore damaging morale was high. The government engaged the resources of Operation Double-Cross. The Germans had recruited undercover agents in England, but they were all found, turned and put to work for the British, sending misleading messages back to their German contacts. The agents were instructed to send full information back on V1s which landed in north London, but almost none on those that landed in the centre of the city. This led the Germans wrongly to conclude that the missiles were off target, and to send them further south instead. Many then landed relatively harmlessly in rural Kent. There was a good degree of quiet satisfaction among the powers that be over this, though politicians were careful never formally to approve the subterfuge. What looked a clever wheeze in central London looked somewhat less great from the perspective of the population of south-east London, to where the V1s had effectively been redirected. Somewhere between one and one and a half million women and children were evacuated in the middle months of 1944, including Elsie Connolly and her four young children. They went to stay with an elderly spinster in Reading who lived on her own in a large house. They only stayed five weeks; by late 1944, the Allied forces had captured the ground in northern France from which the V1s had been launched.

And then came more than 1,300 longer-range V2 rockets, mostly into south-east London. Nearly 3,000 people were killed. In one of the worst incidents, 160 people died when a rocket hit a Woolworths shop in New Cross, eight miles north-west of the Connollys' home in Welling. The last V2 landed in Orpington, eight miles south of Welling, in March 1945, killing one person. By this time the Connollys had a government-issued Morrison shelter in their front room: a rectangular steel cage six foot six inches long and nearly three feet high, where Elsie and the children would sit, crouch or lie through the night when the sirens sounded.

Millions of men were called up for military service – a quarter of the adult male population was in uniform, mostly overseas, by 1945. There were also five million men in reserved occupations – doctors, teachers, engineers, electricians, miners and others – who were not subject to military service because they were needed to keep the war economy going or for other domestic requirements. They included Peter Lewis, Tom Watson and Pat Connolly. Some of them, like Peter Lewis, joined the Local Defence Volunteers established in 1940 when there was a real fear of invasion. Soon renamed the Home Guard, the Volunteers quickly drew in one and a half million men. They are today mostly known as Dad's Army. Subject to little training and provided with almost no equipment beyond a uniform, they have been laughed off in subsequent decades, and are perhaps best viewed, in the words of one writer, as "a laudable if ramshackle form of straightforward patriotism". Pat Connolly had joined the police before the war on a part-time basis. He spent many days and nights patrolling the town centre streets of Welling ten minutes' walk from his house, supporting the air raid wardens and watching for and trying to deal with the bomb damage.

Women were not allowed to fight or fire weapons, but many served in support roles. They were much worse paid than men: in farming, they were given twenty-eight shillings a week, half of which was taken for their room and board, compared to thirty-eight shillings the men were paid. The average wage at that time was eighty shillings (£4). The fighting men were not well paid; factory workers did relatively well.

Jim Lowcock, who had been a part-time soldier in the Territorial Army for much of the 1930s, enlisted in September 1940. He became a gunner in the Royal Artillery. After a period in the UK, from 1942 he served in the armies that liberated north Africa. Allied forces had suffered a series of losses there before 1942, but were reinforced, including with US troops, and were mostly successful after that. The German and Italian forces were finally defeated in north Africa in May 1943. The Allied soldiers, Jim among them, then moved on to Italy, with the invasion of Sicily and, in September 1943, the mainland (initially the "toe" in the south). The advance up the country saw much tough fighting, destruction and loss of life. Rome was eventually taken in June 1944. But there was still more heavy fighting as the Allies moved further north, until the Germans finally surrendered in Italy at the end of April 1945. By then, the Allies had one and a half million men and women deployed in Italy. Jim was still there. He was finally demobbed in November 1945. In the demob papers, his commanding officer described Jim's military conduct as "exemplary". He had "worked consistently well, always showing a ready intelligence and a willing and cheerful nature. Absolutely honest and reliable, with frank and pleasant manner and very sober and respectable habits". Jim was awarded campaign medals, including the Africa Star in December 1943, and the Italy Star. He also received the King's Commendation for brave conduct, and the medal that went with that. He never in the next forty years spoke much about his life as a soldier, consistently dodging questions from inquisitive grandchildren and others. But he said just enough to make clear that, while he had demonstrably done his part, it was not an experience he had enjoyed.

Food rationing began in January 1940, with identity cards and ration books issued to everyone. There was a real fear of food shortages. Before the war 70 per cent of cheese and sugar, 80 per cent of fruit and more than 50 per cent of meat had been imported. But now the country was under threat of blockade and food imports needed to be replaced with home-grown products. Huge areas of former grassland – as well as golf courses and ancient meadows – were ploughed up and planted with wheat, oats, barley and potatoes. People were also encouraged to plant vegetables in their gardens – "Dig for Victory" – and by 1945 allotments, like the one Peter Lewis tended in Ulverston, were accounting for 10 per cent of food production. Similarly, home-kept hens provided more than a quarter of the eggs, including for the Connollys and the Watsons. One of Bill's earliest memories is of feeding tiny chicks at Knotts Mill by hand, their beaks and feet pattering on his skin. A platoon of twenty policemen based in Hyde Park clubbed together to buy eight pigs which they killed and replaced every six months, keeping them in sties made from timber from bombed houses. Beer and tobacco were never rationed. The government needed the tax money they brought in. And people needed some pleasures even in wartime. Rationing was mostly accepted as necessary, but resentment grew as the war years passed and the black market mushroomed to cater to the demands of those who still had spare cash.

There was a thirst for information on what was going on. Newspapers were cut in size because of the paper shortage. Radio was important. Initially the BBC was reduced to one channel, mostly playing recorded music interspersed with announcements. But as early as October 1939, surveys revealed that 35 per cent of people were fed up with that. Propaganda was broadcast from Germany, most famously by Lord Haw Haw on Radio Hamburg. Many people listened but few seem to have been taken in. William Joyce, the voice of Lord Haw Haw, was tried for treason after the war and hanged. But one consequence of his wartime misdemeanours was that the BBC tried harder to keep their audiences by putting on more interesting and enjoyable programmes. From September 1939 the Home Office was writing memos saying things like, "People must feel they are being told the truth". More comedy was broadcast and was successful, especially a long-running series called *It's That Man Again*, which popularised catch phrases like "TTFN" (ta ta for now), "I don't mind if I do" and "'After you, Claude'. 'No after you, Cecil'", an exchange between fictional crewmen on RAF bombers which schoolboys were still repeating to each other in the 1970s. Cinema also kept going, with thirty million tickets a week sold in 1945. Alongside public information films some of the permanent classics made it to the screen in the war years, including Charlie Chaplin's film *The Great Dictator* and the romantic epic of the American civil war *Gone with the Wind*, which followed *Snow White* as one of the first mass hits in full colour.

Much of the horror of the war passed the children by. As Brian recalls:

"I was four years old when the war broke out. I remember it largely as an exciting time with lots of treats. My father was away for most of the war in North Africa and Italy but living effectively in a one-parent family was no hardship particularly in those times as everyone had a huge family and community spirit. The tragedies passed right over the head of the children at the time. We had a big air raid shelter in the middle of the avenue but no-one ever used it. During air raids all the children, neighbours and relatives went under the staircase in the house – this being considered the safest place. After the air raids all the kids would rush around to find the bomb craters and look for any downed aircraft."

Marie's recollection is similar:

> "I remember being taken as a two-year-old in my nightdress to shelter under the Anderson shelter in a neighbour's house. It was communal living; we all had friends our own age in a nearby house, everyone was from Liverpool. There were Canadian soldiers stationed nearby and I remember my aunts going to town and coming back with chocolate and nylons which they had to hide from my dad who did not approve of the fraternising."

After the evacuation, schools ran as normal through the war. Brian's first school was Whiston primary school, which is still there albeit refashioned, and then he went to a Rainhill junior school which was closer to home. As a three-year-old, Marie started at St Mary's Infants, the Catholic school adjoining the church up the road. Her parents knew the teacher, Mrs Donnelly, who said Marie could start when her brother Richard was born in 1942. (One of the Rudd sisters was also generally sent from Liverpool to help out when each new child arrived.) St Mary's was a traditional, somewhat austere set-up; there was a sandpit and a rocking horse but the children were only allowed near them on Friday afternoons.

Stella was enrolled as a four-year-old at St Stephen's Catholic Primary School in Welling, again still there (but largely rebuilt) and also adjacent to the church and a short walk from home. Welling had been a village surrounded by fields before the 1920s. So almost everything there in the 1930s and 1940s was new. Father Nevatt, the priest who had converted Elsie, was an energetic fundraiser and was able to obtain money for a new church building and the school. The senior staff were nuns, led by the formidable and demanding Mother Francis Mary, who is remembered for reducing the other staff to tears (never mind the pupils). Stella followed her two older sisters into St Stephen's, and was herself followed by her brother and younger sister. So Mother Francis Mary impressed herself on the lot of them. None were very regular churchgoers after their mid-twenties. (Mother Francis Mary may later have mellowed; Stella's cousin Andy Connolly, who went to St Stephen's some years later, liked her, at least in comparison to her successor as headteacher. That was Mother Mary Louise, better known as the smiling assassin.)

Following in his father's footsteps, Bill's first school was the Watermillock elementary school. (It didn't last much longer after Bill was there, being closed in 1954 and the building sold, ultimately decades later to end up as an upmarket holiday home which you can now rent by the week.) There was plenty to do at Knotts Mill. Refugee children – possibly from the brief 1939 evacuation of the big cities – and forestry workers were accommodated at the house. There were rowing boats for adventures on Ullswater and plenty of indoor entertainments, as Bill recalls:

> "the radio, piano, a clarinet, a mouth organ, cards, cribbage board, draughts board, other board games and a gramophone and numerous records. The one I recall was a lively hornpipe with the immortal line 'An old maid down in Devon, Said my idea of heaven, Is forty-seven ginger-headed sailors'."

Family life was sustained despite the war. The number of marriages reached an all-time (and never repeated) high in 1939 and 1940, with hundreds of thousands of couples dashing to the altar. The number then fell until 1943, partly because a lot of people had got in early, and then increased again in 1944 and 1945. The war also saw a baby boom, which continued into 1946 and 1947. Marie, Brian and Stella all welcomed new baby brothers in the early 1940s.

Most people heard the war was ending from an announcement on the BBC at 7.40pm on 7 May 1945, declaring that the following day would be a holiday christened VE (Victory in Europe) Day. It turned out a warm, sunny day in London. Crowds thronged the streets, and the pubs ran out of beer.

Two million women without their husbands for years – Polly Lowcock among them – were then bombarded with advice from magazines and newspapers on how to cope with their return. Many soldiers, including Jim Lowcock, did not see their families between posting and demobbing, and contact by mail was sporadic and unreliable. Children who had got used to kissing photos of Daddy goodnight now met the real thing.

Florrie re-joined Tom in Blyth as the war was ending, and Bill then went to his mother's old school, Newsham infants – just a short walk past the pit, along a cinder track parallel to the railway lines which took the coal to the docks and the local power station. In 1946 Tom took a job with a contractor working for Glaxo, the rapidly growing pharmaceutical business, sixty miles south near Barnard Castle. The family moved to the small village of Cotherstone and Bill went to the local school, which he found "a gentle experience unlike that of facing the tough kids at Newsham. We went on nature walks, and did a lot of religion!" And then not much more than a year after that, they moved again as Glaxo hired Tom to work in their new factory in Ulverston. Bill was enrolled in Lightburn Road Junior School, where "a crash course in joined-up writing followed, as I was the only pupil in my year who could only print".

While the end of the war brought a good deal of relief, the material benefits were slow to arrive. Food shortages actually got worse: bread was added to the list of items subject to rationing in 1946. People were increasingly fed up of dull if worthy food. Surveys in 1947 into people's ideal meal revealed that the feast they yearned for started with sherry and tomato soup; moved on to sole; then roast chicken with potatoes, peas and sprouts; and finally trifle and cream, cheese and biscuits and then coffee. For most people this remained a fantasy for years ahead. But things gradually improved. A representative survey of 5,000 four-year-old children in 1950 found they enjoyed a diet that would have amazed their great-grandparents: breakfast was cereal with milk, eggs and bread and butter; lunch involved a lamb chop, potatoes, vegetables and rice pudding; tea included bread and butter, jam and cake; and then there was a glass of milk for supper. For the majority of the population, the main meal of the day was dinner, eaten at lunchtime, but the well-off ate their dinner in the evening while other people were having their tea.

Rationing was in fact one of the triumphs of the blockaded economy during the war years, and it meant, among other things, that your grandparents' generation were the best nourished children in history – taller, leaner and more vitamin-enhanced – even if some of their meals scored higher on nutritional than enjoyment value.

Like continued rationing, the weather and city smog also dampened the spirits. The smog was mostly caused by the huge amounts of coal burned, much of it in domestic fireplaces. Bad weather was a natural phenomenon. The winter of 1947 was bitter, with the coldest February for 300 years, and March seeing snowdrifts up to thirty feet high. Bill recalls that the house the Watsons rented in Cotherstone that winter:

> "had been the nadir of our living standards – no indoor water at all (hand-operated pump in the yard, which froze!) and an old friend, the outdoor bucket loo... [*but then they moved the following year, and*] ... the council house at 53 Well Lane, Ulverston was a step up from our norm, with bathroom, two flushing loos, hot and cold water."

Clothes remained in short supply. Men wore heavy jackets, thick wool trousers and leather boots, and there was no distinction between work and leisure wear. Women's skirts had got shorter during the war, purely because of a shortage of cloth. Garments were bulky and creased, and their owners wore tired faces and bad teeth, topped, for men, with the ubiquitous short-back-and-sides haircut, the main virtue of which was that it helped keep the lice at bay.

It took a long time to remedy the destruction to the housing stock caused by all the bombing. Even by 1951, five million of the country's twelve million dwellings had no fixed bath, and a quarter of the population shared toilets with other families. Many people had moved into new houses in the suburbs in the previous decade. Some of them were destroyed; but much of what was lost was older, less desirable stock in city centres. About 150,000 prefabricated two-bed houses were built in the late 1940s in what was intended as a temporary measure. Elsie Connolly's sister Rene and her husband Reg got one of them, and they enjoyed the internal bathroom and fitted fridge. But it turned out not to be so temporary: they were still living in it in the 1980s. The remaining minority who had not so far been in reach of the national grid gradually got electricity. It reached Watermillock in the 1950s; Tom wired up the inside of the house at Knotts Hill himself with money from a government rural electrification scheme.

Asked in a survey about life's main inconveniences in 1948, people listed poor housing, power cuts (their grandparents may never have known electricity, but once you had experienced it, losing it was a real blow), rationing, queuing and overcrowded public transport. The middle classes bemoaned the difficulty of finding people to do the garden, having to carry shopping home, the laundry challenge and shortages of paper and fuel. People were fed up of state intrusion and control over their private lives. They wanted more of the freedoms and privacy many had enjoyed in the 1930s. They were also tired of the spivs and wide boys who fleeced them through the black market which flourished through the era of rationing.

The years immediately after the war saw important developments in public services, the ramifications of which we still live with now. None was bigger than the creation on 5 July 1948 of the National Health Service. The free-for-all service was trailed in a blaze of cartoon films, pamphlets, adverts and radio broadcasts in the preceding months, but there was some doubt about how it would all pan out. In fact, it was a remarkable success from the get-go. In the first fifteen months, the NHS gave out more than five million pairs of spectacles, nearly 200 million free prescriptions and free dental treatment for more than eight million people. Many women had their babies in hospital without cost for the first time. The biggest early beneficiaries of the NHS were thought to include married women from the working and artisan classes – in other words, people like Elsie Connolly, Mary Lewis, Florrie Watson and Polly Lowcock. Elsie had had Stella in hospital; as had Mary with Marie and Florrie with Bill; but Brian had been born at home in French Street.

The NHS instantly had new problems to deal with. There were 6,000 polio cases in 1949, causing 650 deaths. Swimming pools were closed as a counter measure. Another huge health issue was just beginning to be understood. In 1947 the Medical Research Council began to investigate the rising rate of lung cancer. It had been thought to be related to air pollution. That was not without foundation: Ronald Reagan, who spent part of 1948 making movies in Elstree, complained that the London fog was "almost combustible, so thick was it with soft-coal smoke". But what the researchers discovered, from interviewing 649 lung cancer sufferers across London hospitals was that only two of them were non-smokers. Such was the power of the tobacco lobby that it was still to be several decades before effective measures were taken to deal with the problem, including through the provision of honest information.

Your grandparents have enjoyed lives more comfortable and prosperous than their parents did, and one of the reasons is the expansion of secondary education. In the late nineteenth century, just one child in 300 got a scholarship to a secondary school – and of those that didn't, only the small minority from families who could afford to pay ended up going. From 1907, however, the government provided grants to schools to let more children progress from primary to secondary. This was so popular that competitive entrance tests had to be introduced to ration the places. But that only helped some people. We saw earlier that Peter Lewis and two of the Wilkinson sisters had gained entry to secondary school through an exam, but they were among those whose families could not afford it – and there was no grant for them. The 1918 Education Act increased the school leaving age to fourteen and expanded tertiary education. It also paved the way for more teacher training colleges. Between the wars teachers typically became a bit more competent, because most had been to college, which had previously not been the case. In 1944 a new Education Act created a three-tier system of secondary education: grammar schools for the brightest, technical schools and secondary moderns for the rest.

Grammar schools accommodated one child in five, and entry was determined by the eleven-plus exam, named for the age at which children moved from primary to secondary school. Results day for the eleven-plus was as momentous, nerve-racking and consequential as A level results day is today. The grammar schools proved a passport into the middle classes for clever boys and girls like your grandparents. From Prescot Grammar School and Ulverston Grammar School, your grandfathers found their way into the professions – unlike any of their ancestors in the ten generations we cover in this story. Your grandmothers both went to convent grammar schools.

Their parents realised getting into grammar school was a huge deal: Brian's parents bought him a bike in delight when he passed his eleven-plus exam. Stella's father arranged for her to take the exam for St Joseph's convent grammar school near their home in Welling. Three results were possible: a place, an interview and the suggestion to look elsewhere. Stella got an interview; but the news from that was not good. Persisting, Pat wrote to the school offering to contribute towards the fees, and she was then offered a place. Pat tried to encourage his other children to get the best education possible too, and his son John went to a technical school from where he started successful businesses in refrigeration. When Marie passed the eleven-plus she was sent to the convent school run by nuns in Barrow. Stella Rimington, who was later to run MI5, was there too, a couple of years ahead of Marie.

Brian recalls his time at Prescot Grammar:

> "My school days were pretty undistinguished, winning a scholarship at age eleven to grammar school just after my father was demobilised from the army. My grammar school education is probably best summed up by the fact that I'm not sure whether I or the headmaster was most pleased when I wanted to leave as soon as possible after doing my O levels at sixteen."

In fact, Brian got the third best O level results of all the boys in his school (albeit, as we shall see, in the wrong subjects). The truth is that there was still a good degree of snobbery in the grammar schools, and while the children of the middle classes were supported to fit in, that was not always the case for the minority of those who came from other backgrounds. Many working-class boys left at sixteen as Brian did, and many of them flourished thereafter too.

There remained a clear gender divide even among the grammar school classes. Most of the schools were single sex, for one thing. But while for boys the options after school were wide, that was not true for girls. Those leaving St Joseph's convent in Abbey Wood were expected to become secretaries, teachers and nurses, but above all married. Stella recalls just one girl who went to medical school and became a doctor.

Stella herself was more interested in dance. In 1951, as an underage eleven-year-old (there was a legal bar on children under twelve in professional theatre) and following tense negotiations at the convent, she stood in for a sick classmate as a dancer for the five-week panto season at the Royal Artillery Theatre in Woolwich. The production was *Babes in the Wood*, a panto hardly ever put on these days, and there were five ballet dances and a tap number. Stella loved it:

> "It was very exciting being in the theatre. We young dancers had a large dressing room, we had six changes of costume and were taught to do our own stage make-up. I do remember I had my little box of grease paints. ... We were looked after by a lady called the Matron. On the days we had matinees she took us to a local restaurant for refreshments before the evening performances. ... I was conscious of not being old enough to be there and I was small for my age and one evening the Stage Manager asked whether I was really twelve. I can't remember how I answered him.
>
> We juveniles were paid the princely sum of thirty shillings a week.
>
> After the last night there was a big party which went on until about midnight. My two older sisters thought it most unfair that I was allowed to stay up so late."

The convent in Barrow also had a limited outlook. It was one-form entry, and the quality of education, Marie thought, was not that good. She felt she would have been better off going to the grammar school in Ulverston, but her parents, committed Catholics, unsurprisingly preferred the convent. In the end it worked out for Marie; she liked biology, which was taught in the convent. That helped her land a good job when, as a sixteen-year-old, she wanted to leave. Her sister Sheila, who also passed the eleven-plus, wanted to do more science A levels and left the convent for another school at sixteen.

The social and extra-curricular side of grammar school is what seems to have made most impression on Bill:

> "Having passed the eleven-plus, I moved to grammar school, eventually passing A levels in double maths and physics. On the way I became proficient at cricket and rugby union, mediocre at cross-country running, became a Queen's Scout, sang in the chorus of the school's Gilbert and Sullivan productions, became Deputy Headboy and made lots of good friends."

And from there, in a first in the history of the family, he won a place to go to university. In 1960, just one school leaver in twenty went into tertiary education. These days it is closer to one in two.

As well as school and family life, church played an important role in your grandparents' lives when they were young. Here is Brian again:

> "Evenings were taken up by choir practice on Tuesdays and Thursdays, scouts on Wednesday and

youth club on Friday and Saturday. Sunday was church three or four times depending on whether it was a choral communion or not and Saturdays during the summer often included a wedding in the afternoon for which we were paid the princely sum of two shillings [10p]."

"Colin was the real star in the family as he had a beautiful voice and used to fill the church when there was a soloist at choral services. He was also very good singing leads in musical productions. He was also a Queen's Scout and I remember watching his investiture at Windsor Castle."

In terms of entertainment, Mavis and Brian learned the piano and had to perform duets for family gatherings, which he says did not result in much harmony, either musically or in any other way (and I don't think he's ever been near a keyboard since). Otherwise the radio, cards and board games provided most of the entertainment. "There was so much cheating in the games they often reduced the aunts to tears of laughter and frustration."

The late 1940s also saw the first steps towards a shopping revolution, with Tescos opening a self-service shop in St Albans and Marks & Spencer doing the same in Wood Green. (And hopefully they made good use of the marketing opportunity with younger consumers on the red-letter day in April 1949 when sweets eventually came off the ration, after seven long years. Young Bill Watson certainly seized the opportunity: Archbold's shop, at the end of the lane near Short Row in Blyth, provided him with increasing quantities of mints ("Black Bullets"), aniseed balls, liquorice and something called "Spanish, a stick of root with a flavour all its own". The young Connollys took advantage too. Pat gave them each sixpence a week for sweets after Mass on Sunday – the timing, one imagines, chosen to influence behaviour in church earlier in the day.) Up to then getting groceries generally meant going from shop to shop and queuing in turn for an assistant who gathered the items you asked for. That was fine for people with time to kill and a predilection to chat but it certainly cut into the busy housewife's day. As with other innovations, the new form of shops took time to spread but eventually became almost universal, with the small, proprietor-owned corner shops and newsagents standing out as exceptions.

Football got going again shortly after the war. Nearly a million people a week, almost all of them men and boys from working-class families, would stand on the terraces every Saturday afternoon. Brian and Jim used to go together to Goodison Park to watch Everton:

> "First of all on the tram which took forever and later when I was eleven and got a bicycle we used to cycle ten miles there and ten miles back. The journey back was either euphoric or despondent depending on the result."

Everton at this time were a decent side. They won the League immediately before the war, and then again twice in the 1960s, as well as winning the FA cup in 1966. This was before grounds were all-seated; most people stood on the terraces, swaying back and forward in the throng as the game ebbed and flowed. I remember going to Goodison with Jim and Brian as a seven-year-old, standing on the fold-up stool which they had lugged to the ground, carried along with the crowd and enjoying a game full of incident.

Everton beat Stoke City 6-2 and the local hero centre forward (as strikers were called in those days) scored two of the goals.

There were other pastimes. By the late 1940s John Thomas had a plot of land with large greenhouses, where he grew a few tomatoes. His son-in-law Jim, and very much later still Jim's son Brian, both did the same thing in their times. Brian recalls of his grandfather that "he was a great pigeon fancier and used to race pigeons". This used to be very popular – indeed *Racing Pigeon* magazine has been published every week for a hundred years, though it has a smaller readership now than in the past. The pigeons were driven to a setting-off point, which could be a hundred miles away or more, and then all released together. Magically, they would then all find their way back home. As Brian recalls:

"Sunday morning was spent sitting outside the lofts waiting for the pigeons to return after a race and then my grandfather and his sons went off to the local pub for a liquid lunch. My grandfather was a very small man – under five feet tall – but like many small men he was very aggressive after a few drinks and as I sat outside he was invariably ejected from the pub with a black eye or swollen lip quickly followed by a fighting scrum containing his sons and other miners laughing and joking at the same time. The real fight started when they got home for my grandmother was the best battler of all and her daughters all had very sharp tongues."

Holidays resumed after the war. The working classes now all got paid holiday with their jobs. Half the population left home for a week or so every summer. Camping, which was now a pastime, hiking and cycling were all popular. But most people still went to the seaside. Blackpool, claiming to be "the holiday capital of the world", ran off its boarding houses, fish and chips, donkeys on the beach, ice cream, pier and amusement arcades. It was also now perked up by illuminations, the Tussauds waxworks, the Big Wheel and other daredevil rides, and live shows featuring popular stars like Vera Lynn. Blackpool drew in the Lowcocks, the Lewises and countless others. Herne Bay and Margate were popular with south-east Londoners like the Connollys, who for some years had a caravan in Herne Bay. The year 1950 also saw the first package holiday to Europe. A group of twenty flew to Corsica for a fortnight, with accommodation, meals and as much wine as they could drink, all for just £33. Larger numbers enjoyed Butlins holiday camps, a sort of very minimalist Center Parcs located in seaside towns like Clacton and Minehead, with entertainment for all the family organised by young people in red jackets.

Everyone still listened to the radio, often over meals. There were now twelve million licences, nearly one for every household. Some of the stalwarts of today's radio schedules, including *Woman's Hour* and *Any Questions* first travelled the air waves in the late 1940s. But the dominance of radio had reached its peak. Television was about to take off; in 1949 there were 100,000 sets, but the following year there were four times as many, and it grew like topsy from there.

Everything broadcast was censored. The BBC rulebook forbade jokes about lavatories, honeymoon couples, chambermaids, effeminate young men and women's underwear. But the rules did not just apply to sex: poking fun at religion, politics and physical infirmities was off limits too. Words like blast, hell, damn and bloody, never mind anything of a more lurid Anglo-Saxon origin, were not allowed either. This matched the norms in many families: as a little boy, Brian accidentally provoked dinner table trauma by quipping "Don't be a silly bugger" in response to something someone said. After a stunned silence, his distraught mother laid into Uncle Harry (her brother), the joker of the family, who she concluded must have been responsible for broadening Brian's vocabulary. (Harry had form. In another of his misplaced japes, one year he filled the children's Christmas stockings with cinders from the fire, which unsurprisingly led to them being wafted all round the house, to Polly's fury.)

Trade Union membership increased throughout the period, reaching nearly nine million in 1948. The unions were successful in seeking better terms for their members. Manual workers' average earnings grew substantially. The pay of the professional classes grew a lot too, but more slowly. Unemployment, which had more or less disappeared in the run-up to the war, did not return. Working men were earning £4–6 a week by the late 1940s. After the housekeeping, rent and other essentials, they had money to spare. Tobacco, beer, betting on the football pools, horse races and greyhounds, and the cinema and the annual holiday absorbed much of it.

But by the end of the 1940s, economic strains were becoming clear. The pound was devalued against the dollar in 1949, which helped boost exports, over which there was much concern even though they were 50 per cent higher in 1950 than in 1937. But the devalued pound also meant an increase in food prices, especially as imports grew again after the blockade years of the war. Questions were being raised about the government's nationalisation policy (one curious ramification of which was the renaming of the Fat Director in the Reverend Wilbert Awdry's *Thomas the Tank Engine* books, which appeared from 1945, to the Fat Controller). People worried that nationalisation might be making industry less competitive.

Interest in finding better lives elsewhere grew. In 1945 Gallup found that 19 per cent of people wanted to emigrate. By 1948 it was 42 per cent. As we shall see, some acted on the wish. For others greater opportunities were to be found by moving within the country.

8

Riches: The 1950s

*in which your grandparents leave school, start
work and begin their adult lives.*

The Lowcock family's acquisition of a television
set was prompted by football. The whole street
came to 3 Honiston Avenue to watch the 1953
Cup Final, the so-called Matthews final. It was named
after Stanley Matthews, a butcher's son from Stoke who
became a dazzling right winger and was the first football
superstar. This was his third cup final; he had been on the
losing Blackpool teams against Manchester United in
1948 and Newcastle in 1951. Matthews' reaction to the
losses was down-to-earth: he complained privately to one
of the opposition players about getting a silver medal and
no money. Footballers were famous but not rich in those
days. Now that Matthews was thirty-eight, it was widely
assumed that the 1953 final against Bolton Wanderers
would be his last chance of a cup winner's medal. This
was the first major sporting event to be televised live,
with the audience running to ten million, many of them,
like the Lowcocks, having acquired a set to witness the
romance of the Matthews moment. The dream ending

nearly didn't work out. Bolton were 3-1 up after seventy minutes. But Blackpool scored three late goals, all made by Matthews, the last two of them in the final three minutes, the excitement amplified for viewers by an increasingly hysterical broadcast commentary. The new young Queen handed over the cup, aptly capturing, not for the last time, the feelings of the nation. "Congratulations on a jolly good show," she said.

The 1950s was a decade of unprecedented prosperity: full employment, the consolidation of the cradle-to-grave welfare state, mass (mostly private) housebuilding, a baby boom, low crime, falling infant deaths, and marital stability. Even at the beginning of the decade, most people surveyed thought they were better off than their parents had been. And during the course of the 1950s, the great majority became a lot more prosperous, led by young people, especially women, whose average wages grew more than 80 per cent. Falling raw material prices alongside higher pay meant that basic goods and consumer durables became more affordable. One leading politician observed that the problem now was not jobs for the people but people for the jobs. As a Brighton teenager noted, "once you get to the age of sixteen you can go to any garage or builders or anywhere else and get a job". People from abroad started to arrive to fill vacancies. In 1953, 2,000 came from the Caribbean, mostly Jamaica; by 1956 the number had grown to 30,000.

There was national agreement across the political parties on the big issues: the goal of full employment, the importance of a prominent voice for the trades unions, the hands-on role of the government in managing the economy, the need for some industries to be state owned and the importance of social policies which ensured that the fruits of growth were distributed "fairly". This consensus reinforced conformity and a sense of stability. Public trust in, and the status of, doctors, teachers, nurses and social workers burgeoned.

The economy diversified beyond the traditional industries: banking, shipping, insurance, chemicals, pharmaceuticals, aero-engines and car manufacturing all prospered. Commercial aircraft manufacture looked like it would too, but repeated crashes of the Comet airliners set the UK industry back and it never regained the lost ground. Consumer businesses, like Unilever, Shell and AEI (which made fridges, lightbulbs, washing machines and the like) flourished. So too did ICI, a chemicals giant which hired 6,000 scientific research workers, more than there were in all the country's universities combined.

Material progress was catalogued in newspaper headlines. "We're buying more now," announced the *News Chronicle* in 1953. Less drink and tobacco, more clothes, shoes, cars, household items and better food. Wimpy sold its first beefburger, "the square meal in the round bun". In January 1955, the *News Chronicle* was at it again: "Another Boom Year is Here," proclaimed the headline. That came together with the revelation, reported by an American journalist to her readers, of "markets bulging with every conceivable necessity and luxury". Visiting Stockton-on-Tees, where he had been the MP through the poverty of the 1930s, Harold Macmillan observed that "the wealth and prosperity of the town is incredible", and that "working girls and boys of today are magnificently well-off". Even the staid *Economist* magazine marvelled at "the miracle of full employment without inflation".

This was all reinforced by much better infrastructure. The Town and Country Planning Acts paved the way for slum clearance, the creation of the green belts to protect the countryside around cities, housing estates, tower blocks, shopping centres and new towns, including in places like Thetford in Norfolk. The Wilkinsons in Blyth were among the beneficiaries; Short Row was finally demolished and everyone moved into newly equipped, just-built council properties. The world's first commercial atomic power station was opened in Cumberland in 1956, and was followed by several others. "The atom goes to work for the housewife", said the *News Chronicle*. Nuclear power also helped deal with the horrific smog problem. The coal power station opened in Kingston in 1948 shrouded Surbiton in a poisonous, eye-watering cloud of dusty black smoke until the Clean Air Act of 1956 rescued the situation.

The railways were on the verge of being scaled back, which accelerated the increasing dominance of the car. (Bill inadvertently contributed to that: he had a holiday job one year counting the number of passengers on the Ulverston to Lakeside railway line. Not enough was the – probably pre-ordained – answer. The line was among the large number closed shortly after.) In 1950, British car manufacturers exported half a million vehicles, more than 50 per cent of the global total of car exports. The Morris Minor, originally off the production line in 1948, became the first million-selling car in the UK. In 1958, the first parking meters were set up in London to help manage the growing traffic problem. In 1959, the Mini appeared, intended to be a cheap option for those who had not been able to afford earlier models but accidentally becoming a fashion item, driven by the Queen, Twiggy and the Beatles among others. High-end British cars did well too. The D-type Jaguar took five of the top six places in the 1957 Le Mans twenty-four-hour race.

Roads, finally, evolved to catch up with the traffic on them. The Preston by-pass, opened in 1958, became the first motorway. It was joined the following year by the first sixty-seven-mile stretch of the M1, which would connect London with the north. The M1 came complete with that much-loved and in equal measure hated novelty, the motorway service station, an early example opening in previously unheard-of Newport Pagnell. In 1956, the Supersonic Transport Aircraft Committee established in the Ministry of Supply began the work which eventually led to Concorde.

New inventions and products were unveiled at a dizzying speed. Factory farms for poultry made roast chicken a frequently affordable option for the Sunday lunch of millions. There were coffee bars, with drinkable, caffeinated coffee. Something initially called "Italian Welsh rarebit" appeared. (Pizza, to you.) Windolene, cycle clips, Shredded Wheat, driving gloves, Tizer, Spangles, Scalextric, Marmite sandwiches, *Nellie the Elephant*, indicator wings, plastic cups, sherbet fountains, Edam, Clarks sandals, blackjacks, fruit salads, Dinky cars, Subbuteo, Golden Syrup, instant coffee: all these and more could the eager shopper now acquire. (But not teabags just yet.) And they could do so without making seven visits a week to the grocer and three to the butcher, which was the average before one-stop shopping eased the tired housewife's toil.

Many households acquired fridges and washing machines, previously enjoyed just by the few, and that, together with the spread of supermarkets which permitted the one-stop shopping, hugely improved women's lives as the homemakers. The Hoover factory in Wales, making washing machines, opened in 1948, and the company chairman was unusually prescient in observing that "this machine is going to be welcomed by countless housewives throughout the country". "I can sell more washing machines and these new steam irons than anything else," said another producer; and vacuums, he might have added, because most homes had them too by the end of the decade. Spangles, syrup and Shredded Wheat were no doubt much enjoyed, but millions of the hardest working people (meaning women) in the country could have given them up without losing any sleep – which was not the case with their household machines.

Food choices broadened and eating out became more common. The Shah, an Indian restaurant, opened near Euston Station in 1952; Chinese and Mediterranean cookbooks started to be sold. This was also the dawning of the age of DIY. Dulux paint was marketed from 1953; emulsion appeared, and with it the paint roller. Bright white started to replace dirt-concealing brown.

Also noteworthy was a new machine called LEO, which among other things worked out the wages for 2,000 staff in a bakery, doing the work of hundreds of clerks. Its inventors thought it would "revolutionise the keeping of industrial accounts and records". This was one of the earliest computers, but, it was confidently said, this unprepossessing device was not "one of those machines that imaginative writers like to think may one day get out of hand and dominate the world". Right.

Your grandparents completed their schooling by the mid-1950s. They had benefited not just from being among the lucky winners of the grammar school lottery, but also from better teaching in a broader range of subjects, especially the sciences. Boys in particular found magnets, Meccano, balsa wood, plasticine and Bunsen burners in the labs at school. We observed earlier that science was not prioritised at girls' schools, to the irritation of some of your grandparents' generation. But as we will see in a moment, that did not stop them finding jobs in scientific roles. The expansion of science teaching in schools helped develop skills the new technology sectors hankered after. A levels were introduced in 1951, accompanied by a modest expansion in university education, with slightly more focus on technical skills. In 1900 there were just 20,000 young people at universities; by 1938 50,000; and by 1961 more than 110,000. A group of new technical universities was inaugurated in the 1950s. The tuition and living costs were largely covered by transfers to the institutions from the University Grants Committee, though there were student contributions too.

Bill says he went to university because:

"it was what one did if you had a good brain and the family did not need you to be an earner. I told the careers master that I would become an electrical engineer. I had developed a passion for cars, compounded by being at Aintree when Stirling Moss won the British Grand Prix in 1957."

Having applied to a variety of northern universities – not wanting to be too far from home – he went in 1957 to the Faculty of Technology at Manchester University. The fees were paid by the government, but grants for living costs were means tested, and Tom, now a senior electrical engineer at Glaxo, supported Bill (which delayed, for example, the family's acquisition of a television and a car). The lectures and the labs were in Piccadilly in the centre of the city. In his first year, Bill and ten other students lodged with an Irish landlady next to the Students' Union in Moss Side, a couple of miles south of the city centre. After that he shared an expansive flat with three others in a Victorian villa in the Victoria Park area. Every Saturday afternoon he would go to the football – United one week and City the next, as the home games of the two teams alternated. United were quite a side; they had won the League earlier in 1957, and got to the cup final, as well as getting to the semi-final of the European Cup. But on the afternoon of 6 February 1958 the team plane crashed at Munich, killing many of the star players and injuring more. Bill's bus ride the next morning from Moss Side to Piccadilly was deathly silent, everyone head down into the newspaper to learn who had survived and who had not. By the end of the season the team had slumped to ninth place.

All in all, the 1950s was a good time to be joining the workforce. Brian recalls how he came to his first job as a sixteen-year-old. He had good exam results compared to the other boys in his year at Prescot Grammar. But there was a problem:

"My O level results were notable by my failure in chemistry, which was my favourite and best subject, particularly because I had a job lined up as a trainee chemist with an industrial company in Widnes. So having lost that opportunity I was sent by the local employment exchange for a job interview at Pilkington Brothers Limited, the glass manufacturers in St Helens. I remember clearly sitting in the waiting room with the others waiting